Winning in the Global Market

Winning in the Global Market

A Practical Guide to International Business Success

Bruce D. Keillor

 PRAEGER

AN IMPRINT OF ABC-CLIO, LLC
Santa Barbara, California • Denver, Colorado • Oxford, England

Library of Congress Cataloging-in-Publication Data

Keillor, Bruce David.
  Winning in the global market : a practical guide to international
business success / Bruce D. Keillor.
     p. cm.
  Includes bibliographical references and index.
  ISBN 978-0-313-39832-2 (hbk. : alk. paper) — ISBN 978-0-313-39833-9 (ebook)
1. International trade. 2. International business enterprises. I. Title.
  HF1379.K45 2012
  658.8'4—dc23   2011027584

ISBN: 978-0-313-39832-2
EISBN: 978-0-313-39833-9

16 15 14 13 12   1 2 3 4 5

This book is also available on the World Wide Web as an eBook.
Visit www.abc-clio.com for details.

Praeger
An Imprint of ABC-CLIO, LLC

ABC-CLIO, LLC
130 Cremona Drive, P.O. Box 1911
Santa Barbara, California 93116-1911

This book is printed on acid-free paper ∞

Manufactured in the United States of America

To Rosanne

Contents

Introduction

As the title suggests, this book is about how firms can be a success outside of their home markets. There are lots of compelling reasons why companies of all sizes should consider international operations. At the same time, there are a number of arguments—some reasonable, some not—as to why any given firm would avoid the global marketplace. To some extent the purpose of this book is to dispel those myths as to why an international presence might be a bad idea. The real purpose, however, is to show firms and the individuals who make decisions within those firms, how to successfully get established internationally and how to ensure that success over time.

This book is not just for a company considering entering the global market—although it could certainly benefit from virtually all of the material. It is for firms new to international operations as well as those with an established track record of operating outside their local markets. While written by an academic, it is not an academic work. The goal is to provide real and practical advice. This book is comprehensive in that the contents cover all of the key facets of international business that must be addressed by any company regardless of its previous experience internationally. The book can be used cover-to-cover as a how-to guide for those without international experience or, using individual chapters, as a resource for those firms and individuals with more international experience.

The book is divided into three parts. The first four chapters are designed at putting the reader into an internationally oriented strategic mindset and then contextualizing that mindset through the various aspects of the international business landscape along with the challenges faced by firms operating outside their own legal, political, and cultural environment. The second part—Chapters 5 through 7—address the all-important issues of market selection, market entry strategy, and constructing an international value chain.

The third part of the book continues with discussions of international product strategy (Chapter 8), international promotion strategy (Chapter 9), and concludes with the presentation of a comprehensive toolkit for creating an international business plan (Chapter 10).

What you are about to read is a general guide for success in international business. The mindset, activities, applications, and resources contained here can be applied in any international context by any firm. It is not about a specific region or country. There are a number of other sources that deal with the nuances of the myriad of markets around the world. This book will give you the guiding principles for success in the global marketplace and show you how to apply those principles in a real and practical way. Best wishes for much success in your international endeavors!

Bruce D. Keillor
Youngstown State University

PART I

UNDERSTANDING THE INTERNATIONAL MARKETPLACE

1

The Strategy of International Business

INTRODUCTION

Before we can begin to consider the various assessments and activities that are necessary for success in international business, it is important that we step back and consider the underlying strategic issues of the global marketplace. Too often, both managers and the companies they direct adopt the perspective that international business involves adapting to a "foreign" environment and dealing with all the differences and uncertainties that go along with operating outside of their home market. Certainly there are many challenges, potential threats, and resource issues associated with these international operations. However, becoming too wrapped up in the negative side of moving out of your market comfort zone could easily result in not taking advantage of global opportunities by staying at home or, perhaps even worse, mean entering a market—or multiple markets—with the type of negative mindset that produces negative results.

In order to avoid these pitfalls, we are going to begin our journey to success in the global marketplace by first taking a little time to step back and thoughtfully consider what constitutes the "strategy" of international business. This is not about creating an international strategy for a given business—that discussion is left for the chapters that follow. On the contrary, while an individual firm may construct a strategy that is tailored—and therefore completely different from a similar firm—in any particular international market, the "strategy" of international business that we are going to look at in this chapter is more about adopting an international perspective. That means being able to grasp what it means to be "international" from the viewpoint of any firm, in any industry. That, then, leads us to what makes international business different from just operating in a single domestic market and why this notion of "going global" has emerged in recent years as such an important topic for businesses large, small, and anywhere in between.

WHAT MAKES INTERNATIONAL BUSINESS UNIQUE?

What makes international business unique? The issues that underlie this question go back centuries to the first truly international firm—the British East India Company. What goods to import, what to export, what markets to operate in, what markets to avoid, the logistics of moving product—the list goes on and on. On the surface, it would be easy to say that these are the things that make international business so much more complicated than simply operating in the comfortable confines on your home market.

A closer examination, however, shows that the challenges presented in that list are not really unique to international operations. The issues of what products are necessary to add to a line, and what may have a wider appeal, at the end of the day is not so much a discussion of imports and exports as it is a discussion of product line management. Similarly, what markets to enter and which to avoid is not limited to international business—it is the same basic problem that market segmentation and the selection of target markets focuses on. As for logistics—any business, of any size, is well aware of the importance of the creation and maintenance of an effective and efficient value chain. Further, it is naïve and shortsighted to say that differences in the market environment are the primary characteristics separating international markets from the domestic. All these challenges, and more, are obviously important to consider for any international business, yet they do not get to the fundamental question of what makes international business unique. The answer to this question is straightforward: complexities.

There are three areas where this problem of complexities becomes evident in international business: the market environment, the coordination of domestic and international operations, and the means by which the firm will establish a presence in the host market, or markets. Understanding the complexities of the market environment is not so much recognizing that the composition of the environment is different—that is, the components that make up the market environment do not change, rather the importance or influence those components have in any given market can change. Coordination of domestic and international operations is about the need to manage resources, but also an acknowledgment that different markets may require different levels of resources over time and that this fact must be reconciled in the context of the company's overall operations. Finally, the means by which a firm establishes its presence, or enters another market, can heavily influence both its current and future strategy options. Let's look at each of these in more detail.

THE MARKET ENVIRONMENT

First, consider the issue of the market environment. Later on we will come back to the discussion of the market environment from the perspective of identifying threats. The outcome of that discussion could vary widely from market-to-market and business-to-business. The discussion here will focus on understanding what pieces make up the market environment, how they can influence business activities, and how they might be configured differently to create a unique market environment.

Most experts agree that, from a practical standpoint, the market environment—whether it is international or domestic—is made up of six pieces. These are the physical/geographic environment, the cultural/social environment, the economic environment, the political/legal environment, the competitive environment, and the technological/infrastructure environment. Where the complexity arises is in how each exerts either a positive, negative, or neutral influence on a firm's operations and, most important, how those influences change from market-to-market. The goal at this point in our discussion is not to identify what might be a positive, negative, or neutral influence. Rather, we are focused on one of the unique characteristics of international business—the ever-changing face of the market environment. Like an algebra problem, the market environment comprises a finite set of variables. And like an algebra problem, the "correct" answer is dependent upon how those variables are configured. Identifying which of these environmental variables have the most, or least, impact on a firm's success and understanding that this configuration of the variables does not necessarily hold from one market to the next is perhaps the first step to truly understanding what makes international business unique.

For example, a firm with a perishable product (e.g., agricultural goods) will likely find markets that are geographically dispersed a real challenge—regardless of the demand for the product in each market, while a firm from the same home market with a product that is not perishable (e.g., machine tools) may not see geographic distances to be a serious threat. Alternatively, these same two companies could easily have diametrically opposed views of the threat posed by the technological and infrastructure component of the market environment. A lack of technology and infrastructure may not have much of an impact on consumption of food products, but could very well have a serious detrimental effect on the ability of customers in a market to use sophisticated machine tools.

The trick, as we will see going forward, is to be able to identify in each market the unique configuration of these components of the market environment as they relate to your specific firm. The firm that will be most likely to succeed carefully considers the make-up of the market environment wherever it operates and acts accordingly rather than seeking a "one-size-fits-all" solution to international operations. Coupled with this is the means by which the firm, and those decision makers who represent the firm, approach the market environment. The most successful firms adopt a "directive" approach to the market environment.

What does it mean to be directive? A firm that adopts a directive approach to dealing with the environment, and any challenges or potential threats, is one that adheres to the notion that in many situations business difficulties that arise due to environmental factors can be "managed"; that is, reduced or eliminated through efforts exerted on the part of the individual firm. This perspective tends to run counter to what many of us were taught regarding the business environment, which was that the elements of the business environment are "uncontrollable" and therefore represent restrictions within which we (i.e., the firm) must operate. This is also known as the "adaptive" approach to the environment as firms that take this attitude adjust and adapt their operations around any environmental threat—whether real or perceived.

The issue here is not whether the environment, and its various components, can be controlled or not. Clearly, especially in international business, there will be circumstances where any given element, or elements, of the business environment can be an uncontrollable threat. For example, it is nigh on impossible for a business of any size to exert enough influence to mitigate unfavorable economic conditions and the resulting threats (e.g., volatile or imbalanced exchange rates). The real issue is the degree to which any given company, in the course of either contemplating or engaging in international operations, embarks with an attitude of conformity. In essence what we are saying is: does the firm choose to be "adaptive"—building operations around a reactive mindset—or does the firm choose to be "directive"—approaching operations with a proactive mindset?

Irrespective of any business's international experience it is always the best choice to attempt, whenever possible, to be directive in your approach to international operations. This does not mean that situations that require adaptation will never arise. What it does mean is that the directive firm will be the best prepared to gain, and hold, competitive advantage. The fundamental issue here is for a firm *not* to deal with the international environment from the viewpoint of how to best conform to each of the various pieces constituting that environment. Instead, it is about being able to identify which of the pieces of the international environment are likely threats and then determining what the best way is to deal with each. The best answer may be to adjust and adapt, but by not drawing that conclusion immediately the firm places itself in a position of potential advantage over the competition.

How then to balance these two very different perspectives on the international business environment? As mentioned previously, it is not about an "either-or" approach. Circumstances can easily require any firm to be adaptive. The real answer is under what circumstances it might be reasonable for a firm to be directive—which would mean that before taking an adaptive stance, the firm considers whether or not being directive might be a better alternative.

At the core of this discussion of adaptive versus directive, there are four basic questions that any firm must address in order to determine the viability of a directive approach. First, which, if any, of the components of the international environment represent a substantial threat? The key here is "substantial." Simple differences from one market to the next often do not represent a substantial threat. They are what they are—differences. These differences likely occur every day in home market operations, but are kept in context through the firm's experience in that familiar market. However, when firms extend their operations outside of familiar territory there is a natural reaction to view all differences as meaningful threats. As we will see later, this is a very frequent occurrence when encountering cultural differences. Obviously, a hamburger chain selling beef will need to adapt its menu offering in order to fully capitalize on the demand for fast food in India. At the same time, a firm selling bottled water may find that, while cultural differences exist between Indian, and say British, consumers these differences do not apply to the successful marketing and sales of the product in either of these two culturally distinct markets. A truly substantial threat would be one that was unique to the new market environment *and* had the potential to seriously undermine the company's success. Always remember: differences *do not equal* threats.

The second question to be considered when dealing with the environment in the international market is, can competitive advantage be achieved? Having the ability to change one or more pieces of the environment is certainly an important step in being effectively directive. But to what end? Even if there is a substantial threat in the environment, it makes little sense to engage the necessary resources to manage that threat if the outcome won't result in some form of tangible pay-off—such as a real advantage over the competition. For example, it may be possible to convince a given market that American beer is the best imported beer available. But if the consumers in that market already preferred the local brands, your competitive advantage is limited to only what you have gained over other imports. Hardly a substantial competitive advantage when the chief competitor(s) are local. If the effort won't give you a leg up on the competition, why bother?

The third question to consider is intuitive. By engaging in directive behavior toward a substantial threat, which can result in competitive advantage, will the cost-benefit analysis be favorable? Any good businessperson recognizes that at the end of the day success is measured financially. In working to manage the international business environment it is quite possible to identify a substantial threat and deal with that threat in such a way as to achieve competitive advantages. But at what cost? Every firm, no matter how large, works within the constraints of limited resources. If the amount of effort and resources don't yield at least an equal portion of benefits, then a direct approach to the environment does not make much sense.

Fourth, and finally, there is the question of ethical appropriateness. Never forget that any attempt to manage a host environment is fundamentally an attempt by an outside influence (i.e., your firm) to change the host market/environment. This has the potential to raise ethical issues very quickly. One end of the extreme that obviously falls into the realm of the unethical is actively changing the unfavorable political environment through assassination (e.g., ITT's participation in high-level assassinations in Chile during the 1970s). Others are likely to be more subtle, but ethical dilemmas nonetheless. For example, is convincing consumers in another market that buying from a large, but "foreign," discount store makes them "better" consumers (at the expense of the viability of smaller, locally owned stores) ethical? Is dependence, or even perceived dependence, upon outside goods and services ever ethical? There may be no real answer to these—and a myriad of other similar questions. The important point is to always remember that directive activities impact the people that constitute that other market environment. Ethical behavior in all markets is an absolute necessity for long-term success in international operations.

THE COORDINATION OF STRATEGY OPTIONS

The second place where international business diverges from business activities conducted solely in the home market is in the coordination of domestic and international operations. This is a matter of resource allocation and management. No business, regardless of size, has limitless resources. Such a situation puts a firm at any level of international market involvement in a dilemma. From what source are the resources necessary for international operations to be drawn? In essence the problem is this: success in, what are often unproven, international markets is dependent upon diverting resources from a proven source of revenue—the domestic market. Thus the issue becomes how best to balance operations in these new markets without jeopardizing the revenue stream represented by the home market.

Fundamentally, the choice comes down to three alternatives: adopting either a domestic extension strategy, a multidomestic strategy, or a global strategy. Choosing one of these three options is about determining how the company will approach its chosen international market, or markets, relative to its domestic market. Are operations in the new markets to be essentially unchanged from the way in which the domestic market is approached?, are operational strategies unique to each market to be developed?, or will the firm develop a consistent, singular strategy that can be applied in all markets—including the home market—across the globe?

Domestic Extension Strategy

Selecting a domestic extension strategy is a conscious choice on the part of the firm to try and keep the operational strategies in all markets as close as possible to the tried-and-true methods proven successful in its home market. Essentially, the business chooses to "export" its business model to the new international markets. This means using the same market strategies—product design, promotional appeals, target markets, distribution and pricing approaches, and so forth—as it does in its home market.

For example, a video rental chain may decide that its current business model, built around having and maintaining a physical presence in the form of relatively large stores, is no longer viable given the increasing competition in its home market from other alternatives such as movies-by-mail, Internet streams, on-demand movies, and so forth. It decides that the model is still viable in other markets given that the necessary requirements for its competition to be equally viable do not exist in selected other markets. Whether it be unreliable or irregular mail service, and lack of broadband or high-speed Internet, or an absence of cable/satellite television providers, these alternative markets will not support the competition. Therefore, assuming the international market(s) under consideration (1) have a demand for movies as a form of entertainment, and (2) have the capability to watch the movies, the domestic business model can be "extended" to these other markets.

This means of operating in a new market, using as much of the existing business model as possible, can be extremely attractive from a resource perspective. The domestic extension approach means the business can initiate operations in a new market by simply extending itself. Of the three strategic options for international operations, this choice requires the fewest additional resources—mostly in the area of logistics and logistical support—and is the fastest way to initiate actual "in-country" operations. However, in order to be successful, certain conditions must exist—both in terms of the market, or markets, selected and the firm.

The firm that is successful in employing a domestic extension strategy is one that can accurately assume the conditions that support its current business model exist in the new market environment. Using the video chain example, this would mean more than just the demand for movies and the existence of the necessary supporting infrastructure (e.g., televisions, DVD players). To be truly successful, virtually all aspects of the domestic market must be reflected in the selected international market. Consumers would have to already consider a physical retail outlet as a primary source for video entertainment. Those consumers must be willing to go out of their way, as it were, to rent or buy videos. It must be a frequent enough purchase by the population of that market to be able to support a physical presence. The underlying reasons for making that extra trip—a wide selection of titles, for example—must hold true. And the list goes on. Further, by engaging in a domestic extension approach to international markets, the firm runs the risk of being clearly identified as being "foreign"—which can be a serious problem depending upon the market in question. The domestic extension method is a tempting alternative when resources are tight and it can be a very successful means of operating internationally. However, in order to be effective the characteristics of the market in which it is being employed absolutely must coincide with the characteristics of the market in which it was already proven successful.

Multidomestic Strategy

The second approach, the multidomestic method, is the most resource "heavy." This method is at the opposite end of the spectrum from the domestic extension approach. Where the latter is focused on trying to utilize as much of the existing domestic business model as possible when operating in another market, the former is directed at creating a different business model for each market in which the firm operates. As is the case with the domestic extension approach, its attractiveness is dependent upon the market environment in which it is deployed.

At first glance it is clear that creating an entirely different approach to each and every market would require a significant amount of resources. As the necessary resources allocated to a market, and the time it takes for efforts in that market to pay off, increase so does the burden on the finite amount of resources available to the firm along with the company's ability to sustain current market operations. This begs the question: why engage a market that requires individualized attention when there could be other markets that could be more easily penetrated using a domestic extension approach? The answer lies in maximizing market potential.

The domestic market extension option assumes that there are no key differences between the home and host markets in terms of the firm's business model, product offering, and basic consumer behavior. Although much of these assumptions may be valid, no two markets are ever identical. This means choosing the domestic extension option will likely lead to opportunity costs—either direct or indirect. As we progress, it will become more and more apparent that any time compromises are made the very real possibility of losing some potential customers exists. The challenge is to weigh the extent of the potential opportunity costs against the available resources. In short, effectively coordinating the available strategy options becomes a cost-benefit analysis.

Taking into account that the multidomestic approach is so resource intense, what could make it a reasonable alternative beyond the fact that it will incur fewer opportunity costs? The answer to this question lies in the extent of the actual opportunity in any given market. High levels of opportunity in any single market would suggest that it might be advantageous in the long term for a firm to develop a unique business model for that market. As already discussed, this means consciously committing the required resources. It also means that the firm is comfortable with developing what might, in the end, be a market approach that is so singular once completed that it bears no resemblance to its present business model(s).

A classic example of a multidomestic market approach is Foster's Lager, the Australian beer. A number of years ago, Foster's was faced with a dilemma common to many firms—the need to grow revenues. Unfortunately, also like many firms, it was in a precarious situation in its home market. Foster's was, and still is, positioned in Australia as a low-cost, low-quality beer—which means its only path to growth was to increase revenue by increasing volume sold. And the only way to do that was to compete by lowering the price on what was already a relatively low-priced product in the market. Not an enviable position for any business. So, rather than remaining trapped in this problematic home market position, Foster's decided to consider alternative markets with the idea that the most attractive markets would be ones where the low-price/low-quality perception didn't exist—which would potentially enable its product to be premium, not low-end, priced and by extension reinvent itself.

The key to success lay in the ability to specifically identify what would make Foster's Lager unique once the brand and associated product was free of the preconceived notions of its home market consumers. The obvious product characteristics a consumer might consider when selecting a beer (e.g., taste) were rejected as being too ordinary—that is, these types of product appeals were common in beer-drinking markets around the world. Instead, what the firm decided on was not to focus on the beer itself but to focus on its source. The company's market research showed that consumers in two of the largest per-capita beer-consuming markets in the world—Great Britain and the United States—had a very positive perception of Australia. Thus the decision was made to market Foster's Lager as a premium-priced import in these two markets by leveraging not the traditional aspects of the beer but rather the fact that it was Australian. Hence the positioning in the United States using the promotional appeal "Foster's—It's Australian for Beer" and a similar appeal in Great Britain ("Foster's—Think Australian, Drink Australian").

The result was that Foster's was able to substantially increase its margins on product sales in these two new markets when compared to sales in Australia. But this premium positioning strategy was completely different—and not at all viable—from the way in which it was marketed in its home country. What made this diametrically opposite business model workable? Two things. First, Great Britain and the United States each held huge market potential for the sales of a premium-priced imported beer. Second, while it took time and resources to identify and execute this new business model, the firm recognized that any long-term revenue growth would have to come from someplace other than its domestic market. And there lies the secret to making the multidomestic option successful: identifying a market, or a very limited number of markets, that represent high levels of opportunity and a long-term commitment to those markets, thereby justifying the allocation of the resources necessary to develop a unique business model.

Global Strategy

The third strategy option is the global approach. One of the problems with understanding the global strategy approach is that it is frequently mistaken for a domestic extension strategy. Too often firms are viewed as engaging in a global strategy simply by the number of markets they operate in. Whether or not a business takes a global approach is not determined by the scope of its international operations. Rather, as we have been discussing, it is determined by how resources are applied in host/nondomestic markets versus the home/domestic market.

A true global strategy makes no distinction between home and host markets. Where the difference between global and domestic extension strategies lies is the foundation of the market approach. A domestic extension strategy uses the business and marketing model that has been proved successful in the domestic market. Therefore the foundation to this approach is rooted in domestic operations, which are then duplicated as much as possible in the international realm of operations. In contrast, a global strategic approach is not based on an existing business or marketing framework. Instead, a global strategic approach involves identifying the basic strategic similarities that all markets—domestic and international—have in common in terms of the company's product offering and business model. A single approach to all the markets in which the firm operates is then created with necessary adjustment being made where and when required by individual markets. The result is a "think global, act local" means of operating internationally.

Historically, one of the most common examples of a true global strategy is McDonald's. A number of years ago when McDonald's sought to continue its upward revenue growth it recognized that reliance upon the U.S. market would be too restrictive. So, the decision was made to formulate an international business model. Being in the food industry, it was apparent at the outset that cultural tastes and preferences would require an approach that went beyond the traditional burger-and-fry menu offering. Further, given that the company intended to enter as many markets as possible a multidomestic approach was deemed unfeasible. That meant identifying basic similarities that would hold true for all markets in which the firm targeted for its international operations—both current and future. Finally, as the U.S. domestic market and the international markets would be in constant interaction this single global approach would potentially require changes in the current domestic business model.

The problem then became, what do all customers around the globe—current and potential—want from McDonald's. After much product evaluation and consumer research the conclusion was all customers wanted three things: value, service, and quality. This provided the singular foundation on which to create the global strategy—the "think global" piece. The "act local" portion was then left to translating what each of these three components meant from market to market. Value in the United States was determined to be price-based—hence, the "value meal" menu presentation—while in other markets value was defined not in the context of price, but instead in the context of the McDonald's experience. In this situation, a customer could easily pay a premium price but still consider his experience a good value—much like American consumers pay a premium for sushi, which is essentially a fast food to most Japanese. Similarly, service at a McDonald's meant fast and correct to American customers while those in other markets expected table service. The last piece—quality—to people eating at McDonald's in the United States was found to be heavily weighted toward just the food temperature (e.g., hot/fresh fries) while many of the other markets gauged the restaurants quality by the availability of not only the expected menu offerings but also local food choices.

ENTERING INTERNATIONAL MARKETS

The last area that makes international operations unique from simply operating in the domestic market is the choice of market entry options. This issue will form the basis of much of the discussion, but it is worthwhile to mention it here as entry options are a basic difference that separates domestic and international business.

As was the case with the resource allocation strategy options, there are three fundamental entry choices: exporting, partnerships, and direct investment. While some have suggested that market entry choices are a natural progression starting with exporting, moving up through various levels of partnerships, and finally ending with direct investment in a given market—all predicted on firm experience in international markets—the reality is that each option is viable for long-term operations by companies of all levels of available resources and experience.

The choice to export (i.e., "build it here, sell it over there")—an entry option that will be covered in more detail as we progress—is often associated with the inexperienced firm. In many situations it is the best choice for the firm new to the international marketplace. However, many experienced companies choose to export their products in order to maintain control over their product and enjoy the protection afforded them by their home market's laws and regulations. Additionally, the problem often associated with being labeled a foreign product may not represent a problem as these firms are also able to premium price their offerings based solely on the basis of being an import.

Partnerships, on the other hand, represent a willingness on the part of the firm to give up some control in the interests of closer contact to the host market. These partnerships can come in a variety of forms ranging from licensing/franchising agreements to contract manufacturing up to a full-blown joint venture. The level of resources committed by the firm entering the market may vary, but the goal does not: forming some type of operational or strategic partnership with a local firm in order to tap into that firm's knowledge of the market—consumers, distribution and logistical networks, and competitive experience. The company that engages in some form of partnership runs the risk of ceding control—or even competitive advantage—to a potential competitor in the selected market. But it does this in order to maximize the potential opportunity that exists in that market.

The third entry option, foreign direct investment or FDI, represents the highest level of international market involvement. With FDI, the firm makes a long-term commitment to the chosen market, or markets, through the investment in physical facilities, and often capital equipment. This involves not only large allocation of resources of all types—financial, human, knowledge, and so forth—it also demonstrates a willingness on the part of the firm to take on a high level of risk. Unlike exporting, where markets can be quickly abandoned, or a partnership, which can be dissolved, direct investment means deploying resources and acquiring assets that generally cannot be removed from that market. This high level of commitment means substantial risks are incurred, but for the firm that concludes that the selected market(s) represent significant future opportunity these risks may be worthwhile as the company now is viewed much more as a local firm given that most, if not all, of its activities in that market are now locally based.

To this point, the differences between international and domestic business strategy—from an operational perspective—have been covered. However, there remains one more fundamental issue that must be addressed before moving on to the nuts-and-bolts of conducting international business. That would be the question, is being international really an option?

"TO BE OR NOT TO BE . . .": IS BEING INTERNATIONAL AN OPTION?

Whether or not to engage in international operations is a common question for firms of all sizes. However, given the changes that have taken place in the past decade in the marketplace it may not be an either-or type of issue. A good case could be made that for any firm, regardless of size *and* whether or not that firm is actually involved in international markets, being international has become virtually unavoidable. The nature of the present, and future, business environment seems to suggest that all firms are and will be international to some extent irrespective of their desire to actually get involved in international markets. The most compelling reasons for this lack of choice, when it comes to being international, center on the need for continual growth, forces that require the most successful companies to increase efficiencies and knowledge, and the globalization of both customer and competitors.

The Need for Growth

Most firms desire over time to continue to grow their business and, by extension, revenues. Naturally, to achieve this goal they have traditionally looked to their most operational environment—the domestic market—to obtain this growth. Unfortunately, particularly in the U.S. market, the opportunities for growth are becoming more and more difficult to realize. On one hand, the U.S. market is saturated with product choices—both at the business and individual consumer level. This means that not only is growth within the market problematic, but even maintaining existing levels of customers and revenue becomes a serious challenge. At the same time, other firms from other markets are left with the same problem and choose to move into the U.S. market in an attempt to overcome lack of growth opportunities in their own home markets. Thus the stage is set for U.S. firms to be drawn into competing on an international level without actually leaving the U.S. market. Those that choose to be involved exclusively in the domestic market can expect their opportunities for growth to be more and more threatened not just by other domestic competitors but also by firms from other markets. For any business, the need to grow is real and ongoing. If growth opportunities are reduced at home, firms have little choice but to at least consider entering the international marketplace.

Increased Efficiencies and Knowledge

As the competitive environment takes on more of a global nature—with overseas competitors entering your local marketplace in addition to the increased scope of your own market operations—it becomes imperative for the firm to increase its efficiencies. Obviously this makes you more competitive. What can be—and frequently is—overlooked is that expanding into other markets can assist in the process of increasing efficiencies. Taken from another perspective, this means that the knowledge gained from successful operations in another market can often be used to become more efficient in other markets, including your home market. Each market may have unique strengths such as skilled labor, design expertise, market knowledge, and so forth, which can be applied to advantage in other markets. For example, the Indian market has the distinct advantage of having a large pool of well-educated, technologically sophisticated individuals who also speak English and require much lower wages. Thus, many customer service activities in a wide range of markets can be performed by a customer service team centrally located in India resulting in increased efficiencies.

Another way to look at the importance of increased efficiencies and using increased knowledge is expanding on this notion that the unique requirements of any given local market may be exportable to other markets, thereby creating competitive advantage in other, perhaps all, markets in which you operate.

For example, an established U.S. manufacturer of disposable diapers couldn't seem to get traction in terms of gaining market share in America. The decision was made to expand into the Japanese market as consumers in that market have traditionally been willing to spend relatively large amounts on what they perceive as higher-quality children's products. In the course of starting off in Japan the firm quickly learned that a key change needed to be made to the product—namely the diapers had to be made easier to store without sacrificing functionality. Thus, the slim-line disposable diaper was born—and subsequently moved back to the United States as more households with kids were two-income and constantly on the move. In the end, the firm was able to not only obtain lucrative levels of market share in Japan, it was also able to utilize this new knowledge to gain market share in the United States—something that it had not been able to do with the previous incarnation of the product.

Globalization of Customers and Competitors

The last thing to consider when mulling over the question of whether or not to engage in international markets is the increased globalization of customers and competitors. It is important not to underestimate the increased sophistication of customers given that the global market gives them a much wider range of product choices. This means that all customers, both individual and institutional, have a high level of product knowledge, are willing to consider a broader range of products, and tend to be much less brand loyal than in the past. This means that companies can no longer count on being able to retain existing customers at the same rate as previously. This eroding of home market share stability seems to demand the move to other markets where the local customers also are likely to be willing to accept nondomestic substitutes. Similarly, the globalization of competitors, and the very real possibility that they will move into your home market, also seems to require that firms be willing to engage other markets despite a lack of experience or firsthand knowledge.

SUMMARY

In this chapter we have laid the groundwork for developing a successful international strategy. Before even thinking about the various operational and logistical issues relevant to international operations it is important to consider what makes international business uniquely different from simply operating within the domestic market. From an operational standpoint, three areas stand out in terms of making international business a distinctly different proposition. The business environment, while comprising the same components as the domestic market, becomes incredibly complex as the salient ingredients of any given market environment can vary widely from one market to the other. Further, the management of limited resources must be coordinated through the different strategy options available to the firm. Finally, how the firm will present itself and its market offering(s) must also be determined through the selection of a market entry strategy.

In addition to these issues of distinctiveness when international business activities are compared to those in the domestic marketplace there is also the question of the extent to which global/international activities are a choice. We have suggested here that the need to grow, the ability to gain market share in all markets using the increased efficiencies and knowledge gained through operating in nondomestic markets, and the globalization of both customers and competitors results in all firms being involved at some level in international business. In summary, this chapter is meant to provide you with some thought areas related to international business strategy to lay the foundation for developing a successful plan for international operations.

2

Assessing the Market Environment: Identifying Real and Perceived Threats

INTRODUCTION

The challenge of assessing a new market environment goes hand-in-hand with the process of making the market entry choice. Where market entry is primarily focused on issues such as market selection, timing of the entry, and the appropriate scale of the operations in that market taking into account the firm's available resources, assessing the environment involves understanding the market context in which the firm will operate. This means the firm must obtain not only a general understanding of the market environment in any given market, and by extension how market environments can differ from one to another, but also obtain the necessary knowledge to put those market characteristics into a context that is specific for your individual firm.

As we discussed in Chapter 1, the various components of the market environment do not change when you move from domestic to international operations. The business/market environment always comprises the same fundamental ingredients: demographic, cultural, physical, economic, competitive, political/legal, and technological. The trick is to be able to determine what the underlying nature of each of these ingredients is in a different market and then consider which of these pieces of the environment has the potential to significantly affect your firm's activities in that market.

In this chapter we will take apart each of these components of the environment—with the exception of the cultural environment, which we will look at in even greater depth in a later chapter. Our goal is not only to understand how each of these can impact a firm's ability to succeed but also to address the specific issues within each piece of the environment that must be fleshed out in order to have a clear picture of this new market environment.

THE DEMOGRAPHIC ENVIRONMENT

Understanding the demography of a country is all about having a working knowledge of the population of that country. Population within a market, whether population in terms of individuals or organizations, represents buying units—or demand. However, it is not enough to take the approach adopted by economists and measure demand simply in terms of these numbers. Numbers do not provide a realistic view of the actual demand in a market, or how best to realize that demand. From a practical perspective, this means being able to move past quantity of demand toward assessing quality of demand.

So, understanding a country's population means understanding the country—or for our purposes the market. Knowing the country's population structure allows us to better understand current behavior in the market and, by extension, provide a basis for anticipating that behavior into the future. Strictly speaking, demographics are the objective, factual characteristics associated with individuals that are easily identified and quantified. For example, it is reasonably straightforward to determine gender and age cohorts within any country as these are predetermined characteristics of any individual, which, in the case of gender, presumably does not change (at least those individuals who do change are not a significant portion of the population) or in the case of age changes at a set, predictable rate.

However, from the perspective of a business, a really useful understanding of market demographics must go further. This means being able to identify the important underlying characteristics of the demographic environment as well as how the demography of a market interacts with the other components of the market environment.

Because demographics deal primarily with the characteristics of individuals there is a natural overlap between any discussion of demographics and culture. In order to stay focused, we must remember that in this chapter we want to focus our attention strictly on the demographics of a market and leave the more complicating discussion of culture for later. Therefore, we will focus our attention on overall population of a market and then go one step further and profile a population using the two most powerful demographic characteristics: age and gender. Besides culture, demographics are directly related to the other factors in the market environment. But as a good starting point for coming to grips with a new market, the characteristics of a country's population, and by extension that country's age and gender breakdown, are extremely important for determining what makes that market's business environment unique and what the future might hold for the market.

In short, the approach to a demographic assessment we are going to adopt here will tell you how large and diverse your potential market may be. In addition it will provide you with general information and parameters that will help to guide your decision making before you actually enter a given market. It will also help to identify possible obstacles as well as potential target market segments and create a basis for anticipating the future.

Further, because they are inextricable linked, we will also bring the physical environment into our discussion of population and demographics. Population, and the more developed demographic trends related to age and gender, both influence and are influenced by the physical environment. A country's physical environment consists of things such as geography, territorial boundaries, transportation infrastructure, natural resources, and climate. Keep in mind that this physical environment then directly impacts transportation and the flow of goods, politics, and economics.

Assessing the demographic environment can be approached at two levels—the macro and micro level. At the macro level the issues to be assessed involve the aggregate characteristics of the population. That is, the characteristics of the population of the total number of people in the market. On the other hand, at the micro level, we are looking at characteristics of individuals in that overall population that create meaningful categories, or subgroups (e.g., age and gender categories).

If we take a macro approach to analyzing the demographic environment we will need to consider two basic areas: the physical environment and the characteristics of the market's population as a whole. For our purposes, gaining a meaningful understanding of the physical environment means more than an assessment of the traditional physical environment—it involves putting those physical characteristics into a demographic context. Therefore, we should get answers to the following key questions:

- Where are the major population centers located?
- How accessible are the population centers by air, water, rail, and highway?
- Are there natural boundaries that may impact the movement of your product into the country and then distribution throughout the country?
- What is the climate like and what effect, in any, will that have on your product?

As is likely apparent, our focus on the physical environment is very much about determining the ease at which it will be possible to introduce your product into the distribution network in a given market and, by extension, give your customers access to your product. Clearly understanding where potential customers are, or are not, located is an important first step in helping to direct our efforts in any market. For example, the fact that China has the largest population on earth is not useful knowledge for doing business in

China. There needs to be some direction in terms of where those people—or demand units—are actually located. A closer look at China quickly reveals that there are vast areas of the country in which only very small proportions of the population actually reside. Thus, while China is geographically a very large market, the areas that represent actionable physical market space are significantly smaller than the country itself.

The second area of this macro-level analysis involves understanding the characteristics and trends of the overall population. Here we begin to flesh out the analysis of the physical environment and build a natural segue way to the micro analysis. We need to come to some understanding as to not only how large the reachable population is and the extent to which it is dispersed, but also the nature of that overall population such as the breakdown between urban and rural, immigration/population coming in versus emigration/population going out and the growth rate—that is, growing, stable, or in decline. Once we have completed this macro demographic analysis we now have a more useful picture of the market—one that goes beyond merely viewing market potential in terms of overall population.

At the micro level, the most important universal demographic characteristics of a market's population are age and gender. These can be considered simultaneously. Our purpose is to come to obtain a clearer portrait of the individuals who collectively make up the overall population. When analyzing age the most important questions to answer are:

- What is the current age breakdown of the population?
- Is the population becoming younger or older?
- What influence does the older population have on the overall society?
- What influence does the younger population have on the society now and will that continue in the future?
- How does the age of the population relate to other socioenvironmental factors (e.g., income, education)?
- What are the birth and mortality rates and trends?

Once we have answered these questions we can begin to build a more useful profile of the market. At this point, we have specified the overall market potential and the extent to which that potential may change over time. The final piece to this micro-level demographic analysis is to understand the gender composition of the population looking at:

- The ratio of males to females
- The percentage of females of childbearing age and the factors that might affect childbearing (e.g., health care, nutrition)
- Identifying any societal roles that are strictly defined by gender

Remember, while it might be tempting to more deeply explore character-istics of the individuals that constitute this population, at this point we are only interested in assessing the overall market environment from the per-spective of a business decision maker. We will address more involved issues related to individuals in another market in a later chapter dealing with cul-ture and the social environment.

THE ECONOMIC ENVIRONMENT: WHERE'S THE MONEY?

As your strategic focus shifts toward global markets, you will need to iden-tify whether or not the market you are planning to enter can sustain your firm and its product. This sustainability is closely tied to the demographic envi-ronment. Understanding the demographic composition of a market means being able to map out the location and characteristics of potential market segments. Where these consumers, or buying units, are to be found and the commonalities that bind them together as a viable market segment is an es-sential first step in evaluating the potential of a market. However, this demo-graphic assessment only addresses the characteristics of individuals as these pertain to where they are and who they are. Using just a demographic assess-ment does not take into account the crucial issues related to the economic environment—those being the quantity and quality of demand.

It is widely accepted that the economic condition of a country is perhaps the most important component of the business environment when firms begin to seriously think about international opportunities. Thoroughly as-sessing the economic environment is especially important when you and your firm undertake the process of identifying any prospective markets and, by ex-tension, try to get a grasp on both the real and perceived differences between your home market and those of potential targeted markets.

A key factor in all of this is the actual purchasing decisions about how much and how frequently consumers in the market in question might buy of your product. This purchase decision is clearly directly impacted by their purchasing power or, put another way, their economic ability. It may well be that only small groups within a country, or market, have the economic abil-ity to purchase your product. The question then becomes, is this group suf-ficiently large enough to offset the costs of operating in that market? Further, how stable is this demand? At the same time, is the country moving toward a more advanced stage of economic development where the purchasing power, and the competition, is expected to dramatically increase in the near future?

Such a situation has the obvious benefit of obtaining more potential rev-enue as the economy develops but also contains the possible threat of having to work harder for this revenue as competition is drawn to the market's potential. This would then raise the strategic question of what is more important to you and your firm: an immediate short-term approach with limited, but perhaps more easily attained, outcomes or a longer approach with greater profitability potential but also greater competitive challenges. These are the strategic issues that the assessment of the economic environment is designed to deal with.

When it comes time to compare potential countries in terms of business potential using an economic perspective, you must consider a variety of factors such as the general economic outlook, employment levels, amount and distribution of income, growth trends, and so forth. There are a myriad of potential economic statistics, trends, and indicators that might have value when conducting an economic assessment.

An economic assessment is very much about identifying what activities in the market form the foundation for its economy. Knowing what constitutes the primary economic activities within a country goes a long way in helping you to determine not only what types of products are likely to be in the most demand, it also helps to draw conclusions regarding the stability of the market (quantity vs. quality of demand).

For example, countries that are considered to be less economically developed will be focused on activities centered on basic existence such as agriculture. A basic framework for matching the level of economic development in a market with the pieces that are important to a businessperson, rather than an economist, involves thinking about economic development in a given country as being at one of three levels: primary, transition, or tertiary. In a primary economy activity is almost exclusively what an economist would call *subsistence*; that is, producing products that are used by the population for its own existence.

This would likely mean two things. First, the products being produced would be retained and consumed in that market and second, the scope of opportunity in the market could be limited. It seems clear that a market where the activity is almost exclusively directed at survival would not have a substantial and sustainable level of demand for luxury products more associated with developed markets but that does not mean there is no opportunity at all for outside firms. There may be considerable opportunities for outside firms to provide products that enhance the efficiencies of this primary economic activity—in other words a firm that brought in hybrid seed, fertilizer, irrigation equipment, or farm machinery might find a primary economy to be exactly what it is looking for in an international market while the firm seeking to export advanced consumer electronics like plasma TVs would find this market to be lacking in attractiveness.

At the transition level, an economy is beginning to move beyond subsistence activities toward creating value-added products. For example, taking basic natural resources such as timber and using the resulting product not just for basic construction but turning that product into something finished (e.g., lumber) that has a higher value and could garner demand that extends beyond its own market boundaries. This expansion of economic activity also means an expansion of opportunities in these markets. First, a wider range of products being produced means there is potential for those businesses producing these products to require more and better products that can enhance their overall efficiency. Second, as the products in the economy move toward having larger and larger elements of "value-added" to them there is a need for more specialized labor input. With this increased specialization in the workforce there is typically a corresponding increase in the wages that must be paid to individuals—the result being an increase in buying power for consumers in a market where there may not be a local source for more sophisticated consumer goods. Thus, the environment may be very conducive for the successful introduction of nondomestic goods.

The third, and highest level of economic development, is a tertiary economy. These would also be known as a developed economy. In a tertiary economy most of the local economic activity is service-based products. Generally, the tertiary economy is associated with high levels of income that, in turn, would suggest a high level of quality of demand for a wide range of all types of products. As a result of these economies concentrating internal activities around high-level products (e.g., technology) the opportunity for providing the full spectrum of consumer and industrial products exists in these markets. However, in the past few years we have learned that high levels of economic activity do not also mean high levels of economic stability. It can be argued that these tertiary economies, while being associated with high levels of income (i.e., ability to pay or quality of demand) can also be very vulnerable to outside shocks that can dramatically, and in a short period of time, reduce the demand in that market.

So, given the complexity of performing an economic assessment we need to come to grips with the questions that must be answered. These questions deal with the level of development, demographic transition status, the country's economic system, the country's attractiveness as a revenue generating market, and consumer purchasing power.

- What is the country's level of economic development (primary, transition, or tertiary)?
- If the country is at the primary level, is it showing rapid population growth?

- If the country is at the transition level, is population growth slowing?
- If the country is at the tertiary level, is there little natural population growth and is there any significant population growth that can be attributed to outside sources (e.g., immigration)?
- Is the economic system predominantly an open system (e.g., free market)? If so, what are the rules/regulations governing it?
- Is the economic system predominantly a closed system (e.g., government controlled)? If so, is there any room for entrepreneurship?
- How much, if any, flexibility is there to operate within the existing economic system?
- Does the government view its primary role as a facilitator or provider?
- How does the government deal with the concept of fair competition?
- What are the primary sources of economic activity?
- What metrics (e.g., gross domestic product) are used to assess the strength of the economy?
- What is the quantity and quality of demand for products and services?
- What is the availability of raw and component materials?
- What is the availability of labor and capital?
- What does the consumer income distribution look like for the country?
- How would quality of life be assessed in the country?
- Where are the consumers with the greatest amount of purchasing power located?
- Is the purchasing power limited or is it expected to grow across different classes of consumers?

THE COMPETITIVE ENVIRONMENT

One of the more misunderstood components of the international business environment is the competitive environment. It is easy to assume that the primary source of your competition will be from firms based in the local market in which you intend to operate. The reality of the current global economy is that your competition can come from one of three possible sources (local, your market, and other outside markets)—and it is quite possible that the largest competitive threat is not from the local firms.

Consider the logic of automatically assuming that local firms will be the biggest competitive threat. It is easy to see why a firm might conclude that local competitors represent the biggest threat—that would certainly be a real possibility if one was entering a fully developed market. However, the most attractive markets are often those that are developing to some extent. The logic that follows is that there is substantial competitive opportunity in these markets as the local firms cannot keep pace with the rate of economic growth. What is missed, following this line of logic, is that in order for this scenario to hold the single outside firm must be the only one that recognizes opportunity in that particular market—a dangerous assumption.

Basic economics tells us that when opportunity arises in a market that is the signal for firms to enter—not just your firm, but all firms. Thus, it is possible that local firms will ramp up their competitive activities. It is equally possible that firms outside of the local market will recognize the business opportunities. As previously mentioned, the other possible places your competition can originate would be from your own home market or from other markets outside of the targeted local market or your own home base of operations. For example, a U.S. firm entering into operations in Malaysia might face competition from indigenous companies, other U.S. firms, and other Asian or European firms as well. The new global marketplace is often referred to as being *hypercompetitive*. That means not only are there more markets of opportunity, but there are more competitors. Understanding the source, or the market of origin, of your competition is the important first step in assessing the competitive environment. Determining where the firm, or firms, that represent the biggest threat are based involves a two-step process: identifying their market of origin (local, your home market, or other markets) and then assessing any source/market-of-origin advantages they might enjoy.

While there may be a variety of advantages afforded to your competition, depending upon the market from which they originate, generally these so-called source advantages fit into one of four broad categories. First there are the potential advantages given to local firms in the form of subsidies or other political benefits. Provided your primary competitive threat is these local firms, any advantages that enable these firms to avoid operating in a fully competitive environment become problematic for your firm's operations.

The second and third categories of source advantages relate to firms from other markets; that is, not local firms nor those from your home market. As was the case with the first, these are fundamentally politically oriented source advantages. However, the nature of those advantages are very different. The second category of source advantages involves an absence of trade barriers—discussed more in the next section—that would give firms from those outside markets an enhanced ability to move product across joint borders. This would be a clear operational advantage. The third category involves not facilitating the movement of product but the movement of profits. These source advantages often come in the form of exchange agreements, or other types of special treatment when it comes to repatriating revenues.

The fourth, and final, source advantage would be those enjoyed by other firms from your home market. The first three categories of source advantages have a political element that more often than not means that if they exist for other firms originating in your home market they can also be an advantage for your firm—at least under the level playing field assumption that the U.S. government tries to propagate. This fourth category would be an advantage extended to other home firms by the local market. These very often come in the form of some type of ownership arrangement (e.g., the creation of a subsidiary or another form of joint venture) through which the participating firm is essentially treated like a local firm. Regardless of the source advantage(s) that might exist, assessing these before evaluating where any competing firms may, or may not, have actual competitive advantage will enable you and your firm to better focus your efforts and not waste time assessing the potential competitive advantages of firms that are not your actual main competitors.

Once you have identified which firms to assess, then it is time to conduct the actual competitive advantage assessment. Whereas the first step in conducting a competitive analysis deals with "who" the competition is, the competitive analysis deals with the question "why"; that is, what specifically makes them a competitive threat. The natural segue way is to start by projecting your identification of the competition from the present into the future—a true strategic perspective recognizes that the firms that make up the competition in the present are not necessarily the competitors of the future.

For example, in the past companies who produced laptop computers might be correct in assuming that their most important competition was from other laptop computer manufacturers. However, the rapid development of wireless technology and the advent of smart phones means that the competitive set has shifted toward mobile phone producers and providers. Why is this important? Clearly, being able to identify any shift in your competitive set is vitally important. However, there is a more important issue here—by focusing too much on singling out competitors solely based on its actual product type a firm can easily lose sight of what its product is to its customer.

The customer is not terribly concerned with what the product is—she is more concerned with what she gets from the product (i.e., the product's "value"). People who buy laptop computers do not buy computers; they purchase a product that will assist them in processing and disseminating information. The mobile phone becomes a very viable alternative for them given the size and cost advantages. This becomes of particular importance in international markets when we take into account the fact that consumers in other markets could easily be buying your product for a very different set of reasons from that of your home market consumers. So the first step in any competitive analysis is to carefully consider what it is that your company has to offer—not the product category but what the customer gets from the product. In other words, a value-oriented assessment of your product conducted from the perspective of the customer.

Once we know what it is we have to offer the customer we then need to come to some determination of the extent to which our competition will fight for market share in the markets we have targeted. We do this before getting too far into a detailed analysis of competitive strengths and weaknesses for one singularly important reason—if they are not willing to fight for market share then we may not need to invest significant resources in making that market profitable. This raises the question—why would a firm go into a market without full commitment?

The answer is straightforward: some firms, particularly large multinationals, rely heavily on their worldwide brand recognition, which means entering a market to them is simply making the product available to the local consumers. If the product catches on, or if there is a reasonable return on their efforts, then they are content. Historically, Coca-Cola has been confident of the power of its brand in all markets around the world. Pepsi has shown that in some markets (e.g., Eastern Europe) it can gain a majority of market share by exerting extra effort—Coke simply does not see that pay-off in committing the resources necessary to beat Pepsi in those markets. The result is that there is no need for Pepsi to take Coke on head-to-head and, therefore, no need for a full competitive analysis as its focus can be simply on building brand equity and exclude any real discussion related to why Pepsi products are better than Coke.

So what do we do if the competition takes a more conventional approach and is committed for the long haul to the same market your firm intended to make profitable? This is where your firm must engage in addressing the traditional issues associated with a competitive analysis—namely, the competition's strengths and weaknesses. This process can quickly devolve into a quasi-scientific exercise. This happens for several reasons. It is easy to assume that the only way to accurately assess the competition is through an objective assessment of its products and firm operations. An objective approach can be quantified and therefore more easily analyzed. Using objective facts means there is some basis for ongoing comparisons. The list could be easily expanded.

Unfortunately, what this objective approach does not take into account is the most important issue—what do the consumers think? A theme that permeates success in business, especially international business, is that perception is reality. If consumers believe it—that is, they act on what they think they know rather than objective facts—then they act on those beliefs and that perception steers the marketplace. If American consumers believe that German cars are more reliable than Korean cars (which objective facts show is most certainly not the case) then we will pay a premium for German cars and the Korean manufacturers will have to battle this negative image regardless of the facts.

How, then, do we assess these subjective strengths? It's easier than it might appear. Perceptual strengths are characteristics that the competition actively attempts to build up in the minds of consumers. In order to accomplish this it must openly communicate those strengths in the marketplace. Identifying the strengths that the competition has singled out as making its firm and product unique is as simple as parceling out the characteristics of its offering it is pushing in the market. Recent BMW ads have emphasized the singular uniqueness of its cars while Kia and Hyundai try to convince the U.S. car-buying public that their products are of the highest quality but not the highest price. The strength of the competition can be relatively quick to deal with—because it doesn't want to hide its strengths.

Weaknesses, on the other hand, can be a little trickier. No firm wants to telegraph what it, or its customers, see as a weakness. Not only would that open up the possibility of having those weaknesses exploited by the competition (read: you) but it is not unheard of for a firm to identify weaknesses internally that are either not recognized by the external market or not considered to be a real weakness. Making too much out of these will only serve to focus negative attention on the company and its product(s). This means the approach to weaknesses is, assuming they can't reasonably be fixed, to hide them.

If the potential opportunity these weaknesses represent is hard to objectively identify then what can be done to exploit them to the advantage of your firm and its products? One obvious path is to attempt to objectively identify the weaknesses of your competition. This approach represents a number of difficulties. First, it is expensive and time-consuming to engage in the activities necessary in order to truly identify the weaknesses of another firm and its product offerings. Another problem would be that what you and your firm consider to be weaknesses may not be seen as such by the marketplace—if customers don't see the weakness or simply don't care there is precious little to exploit. Last, objectively identifying shortcomings in another company could, in the end, present your firm in an equally bad light—if you are going to be truly objective in your efforts you won't have any control over the outcome. So if dealing with the competition's shortcomings is so hard to accomplish in any kind of objective fashion, what can we do? The answer is simple: instead of identifying real weaknesses we make them up.

Let's pause here for just a second. Clearly this statement—taken at face value—has some real ethical implications. Therefore we need to be clear: there is no suggestion that anybody or any firm engage in lying to the public. Beyond just the fact that such behavior is not only unethical but potentially illegal, that kind of thing is not what we want ourselves and our company associated with. What, then, does "make them up" really mean? This approach simply recognizes that weaknesses are in the mind of the beholder. Put another way, exploitable weaknesses are those that are perceived as such by the market and the customers that make up the market. The most effective means of leveraging exploitable weaknesses among your competition is to manipulate the market's perception of its offerings relative to your own.

By creating a perception in the market that you excel when it comes to certain product features, firm characteristics, operational approaches (e.g., excellent customer service), or any one of countless other things customers seek out—things that you are careful to emphasize as being your own particular strength—you will create the belief in the market that you are better than the competition. Or taken another way—the competition has obvious areas of weakness that make its offerings less attractive than yours. Perhaps this is a subtle distinction between publically emphasizing strengths and exploiting differences. However, if we only emphasize the strengths of our firm and what it has to offer we place ourselves in the position where the market draws its own conclusions. It is much more advantageous for us to take the extra step and not only demonstrate our strengths but also emphasize how that makes us better than the competition (i.e., highlight what it doesn't do as well—its weaknesses). This allows us more control over the outcome—that is, the perceptions of the marketplace—and results in us gaining competitive advantage.

This leaves us with one more issue related to the competition, and gaining competitive advantage, which cannot be ignored—how do we deal with changes in the competition's strategy? Changes in the competition's strategy can be disconcerting. We establish our own strategies with an eye to beating our competitors. When these competitors change course it is easy to begin to question our own strategy. The most obvious question that arises when this happens is what do they know that we don't? The correct answer is: maybe nothing. Never assume that your competitor has a crystal ball that accurately sees the future. Simply assuming they know more than you will not only cause you to potentially change a perfectly acceptable strategy, it will put you in a position where you are always behind your competition because your approach is based on reacting to its strategic moves. It is more appropriate—before reacting to any change of course adopted by the competition—to seriously analyze not only why it might be making these changes but what the possible outcomes (notice we said "outcomes" plural) might be. They may not necessarily be positive outcomes.

An example of this type of approach to changes in a competitor's strategy can be drawn from the U.S. tire industry in the 1990s. Then, as now, Goodyear Tire and Rubber was the single largest tire manufacturer in the world. Over the years, Goodyear was able to do what few companies have been able to accomplish—premium brand what is essentially a commodity product. It did this through its established dealer network that meant exclusive aftermarket sales only through a Goodyear dealer. While this approach created significant brand equity for Goodyear, it had two major drawbacks: first, it meant that a substantial amount of the profits from aftermarket tire sales had to be shared with the dealers and second, it limited the company's sales volume. In Goodyear's search for more growth in sales, and by extension profits, it decided to expand its retail distribution base. More to the point, Goodyear decided to allow sales of its tires in large retail outlets, most conspicuously Walmart.

The reasoning behind this bold move is pretty obvious. Large retailers not only have the potential to move much greater number of tires in any given time period compared to the dealers, but this strategy also allowed for streamlining of the distribution channel (fewer retailers to deal with relative to the number of tires being sold) and had the potential to increase profit margins through a more efficient and direct distribution model. The logic seems inescapable. Yet, Goodyear's larger competitors such as Michelin and Bridgestone did not, at that time, immediately follow it into the discount retail market. Why would these firms who were very desirous of getting any kind of advantage at all over Goodyear not respond to a move that seemed destined to result in Goodyear increasing its market share and profits in the United States?

The answer lies in those other firms' analysis of not only the potential success of Goodyear's strategy change but also the possible negative outcomes of the firm's new direction. They determined—as it turned out rightly so—that Goodyear might achieve gains in sales volume but would not increase its market power or profits. The competition's conclusion was that by moving away from its established dealer network Goodyear would damage the brand equity it had so carefully constructed over the previous decades. This would mean lower profit margins as the price that it could charge for tires would be lowered as customers became more reluctant to pay a premium price for tires that were being mass-marketed through discount stores.

This was exactly what happened. While Walmart may be many things, it is not associated with premium brands or premium prices. That meant that Goodyear tires took on the perceived qualities of a discount, not a premium, brand. Further, this really eroded the company's sales through the dealer network—the foundation of the firm's success—as not only customers purchasing Goodyear tires were more inclined to do so at a discount but the dealers saw no incentive to push Goodyear tires because in their minds the large firm had abandoned them. The difficulties were further compounded when Goodyear learned—as do many companies—that large retailers, and Walmart in particular, tend to place a great deal of pressure on their suppliers. The end result was that Goodyear was able to move much larger numbers of aftermarket tires but at the cost of its brand equity and profits. The moral of the story is: no matter how old and established the competition it can still make poor decisions. Consider carefully all possible ramifications of its new direction before you follow suit.

What questions, then, need to be answered in order to engage in a meaningful assessment of the competitive environment? These questions are as follows:

- Where does your primary competition come from (i.e., local firms, other firms from your home market, or firms from other markets?)
- What source advantages do these firms enjoy? Subsidies for local firms? An absence of trade barriers and/or the existence of revenue benefits for firms from other markets? Subsidiary or joint ventures advantages for other firms from your home market?
- Who exactly is the competition now? Will it change in the future?
- How important to your competitors is the market in which you intend to operate?
- What are the competition's unique strengths? Are these seen as such by the local consumers?
- What are the competition's exploitable weaknesses?
- What are the likely future changes in the competition's strategy and what will be the impact of those changes?
- What are some of the possible outcomes of any change—future or recent past—in the competition's market strategy?

THE TECHNOLOGICAL ENVIRONMENT

Assessing the technological environment allows us to look at a country as a prospective market that may, or may not, be ready for your product(s). It is important to keep in mind that although your actual product itself may not have any substantial technology requirements, its supply chain, marketing activities, sales, distribution, and customer service might.

The term *technology* can be somewhat misleading when we take into account the fact that there are different levels of technology. For example, things such as equipment and machinery are considered to be "hard" technology—or more traditionally a physical plant. On the other hand, software and management techniques are considered to be "soft" technology. Likewise, when the level of technology in a country is less developed, relative to your home market, that market is usually viewed as a labor-intensive technological environment while a more advanced technological market is termed to be capital-intensive. It is important to keep in mind that any changes in the technological environment of a market can have truly dramatic effects on the development and implementation of a successful business model.

At the same time, it is important to recognize that the target country's level of sophistication with technology is not necessarily the same as the country's level of technological development. Advances in personal technology—such as smart phones—mean that it is not uncommon for the business environment to lag behind the consumer population. Therefore we need to think about whether or not technology is available and used not only by businesses but also by residents in the market and the availability of what we might consider to be common technology such as personal computers, mobile phones, and the Internet.

Finally, the transfer of technology is also a critical factor in understanding the technological, and therefore the overall, business environment. Technology transfer has become extremely important both between and within countries due to advances in global communication and the resulting economic dependence of countries. The transfer of technology has allowed lesser developed countries to compete on a regional and global basis and, more important, has enabled these countries to integrate innovative products into their markets at a previously unheard-of rate. Not only has this increased the level of product selection and sophistication, but it has also improved living conditions and productivity in many of these markets through technology transfer in areas such as agriculture and health care.

Organizing an assessment of a country's technological environment would then center around four areas: (1) level of technological education, (2) level of technological advancement, (3) technological infrastructure, and (4) level of technology transfer. Questions that must be addressed in each of these areas include the following.

Understanding the Level of Technological Education

- What is the educational level of the population?
- Is advanced technology taught at all levels in the educational system?
- Is technology available and accessible throughout the educational system?
- What is the country's attitude toward technology?

Understanding the Level of Technological Advancement

- What is the country's level of technological advancement?
- Is technology relatively new?
- Is technology highly controlled? Who controls it?
- Is it accessible to the entire population?
- How expensive is it?

Understanding the Technological Infrastructure

- What characterizes the technology infrastructure?
- Is there an inexpensive and reliable supply of power?
- Is there a sufficient and evenly distributed number of the necessary components (e.g., towers, hardware, Internet providers)?

- How difficult and expensive is it for businesses to replace and/or update equipment?
- Does the country have a plan or vision for technology in the future?

Understanding the Level of Technology Transfer

- Does the environment encourage technology transfer?
- Is there a single or limited number of standard systems in the country (e.g., operating systems, communication software)?
- Are these systems compatible with those in other countries/markets?
- Are there logistical barriers to hard and soft technology transfer?
- Are there any legal barriers to technology transfer?
- Are there differences in equipment standards and protocols?

SUMMARY

In this chapter we looked at some of the key areas of the international business environment. Leaving the cultural and political components for later discussion, the focus was on the demographic, economic, competitive, and technological elements of the international business environment. In each case we developed a conceptual understanding of the issues involved and concluded with a set of questions that your firm can utilize in order to begin the process of assessing these areas. The demography of another country, or market, involves having a working knowledge of the population, or customers, of that country. Assessing the demographics of another market can be approached at the macro level (the aggregate characteristics of the population) or at the micro level (the characteristics of individuals or subgroups of individuals in the population). The economic environment is closely tied to the demographic environment. Understanding the economic element in a market enables your firm to have a clear picture as to the quantity and quality of demand as well as the all-important issue of market stability and opportunity over time. The study of the competitive environment helps your firm to better focus its efforts effectively by identifying your real competitors as well as the advantages those competitors might enjoy in any given market. We also introduced the notion that it is the value the customer receives from the product and not the product type that defines your product. Finally, we looked at the technological environment and the important questions related to technological education, advancement, infrastructure, and technology transfer.

3

Assessing the Political Environment: Beyond the Marketplace

INTRODUCTION

The political and legal environments tend to get lumped together in any discussion of the overall international business environment. Although they are inextricably intertwined, each is very distinct in the way it must be approached in any effort to reduce its impact and, by extension, increase firm efficiency and effectiveness. The legal environment represents the laws, regulations, and other rules that constitute the structure dictating how business is conducted within a market—in other words, the rules of business. The political environment, on the other hand, involves both the players and the processes by which this structure is created and evolves. If a firm adopts the directive approach to dealing with its environment then the focus of its activities will be more centered on the political rather than the legal environment.

The reason for this is straightforward and has nothing to do with any suggestion that the legal environment is not a key influencer of firm success. That is not the case. The reason the directive firms tend to focus its attention upon the political environment is that it is easier to proactively manage the process-oriented nature of the political environment than it is the structure-oriented legal environment. Put another way, paying attention to the political environment provides more opportunity to head off any potential threats that might later manifest themselves in laws and regulations than does attention paid to already codified laws and regulations—influencing the process is much easier than altering that which is already established.

WHAT IS THE POLITICAL ENVIRONMENT?

If we are to approach the political environment with at least the anticipation of being able to manage aspects of it to the advantage of our firm we must have a clear idea of how this aspect of the international business environment is defined. While the working definition of the political environment we will use here might not be wholly embraced by a political scientist it is useful in helping us understand what we are dealing with—or attempting to deal with. For our purposes we will define the political environment as follows: all non-market individuals, institutions, or organizations within a country that have the ability to control the operations of a firm in that market.

In order for a definition to be useful it must provide guidance and direction; after all we are not involved in an academic exercise, rather we are seeking to gain practical, useful knowledge that can be translated to international business success. With that in mind, let's dissect this definition.

The most important piece of the definition, indeed the whole reason to consider the political environment in the first place, is the second part of the definition ("have the ability to control the operations of a firm in that market"). There is little point in spending any time or effort on the political environment if it doesn't have any potential to influence our business activities. So, let's accept the fact that we are concerned with the political environment because it has the potential to negatively impact our success. Our attention then shifts to the first part of the definition ("all nonmarket individuals, institutions, or organizations within a country").

How does this piece become significant? *Nonmarket* refers to the business environment outside of any transactions. Therefore, when we are dealing with the political environment there are large pieces of the international business environment we are specifically not considering such as customers, competition, suppliers, and so forth. The nonmarket environment is outside the traditional microeconomic environment and its related components. The individuals, institutions, and organizations then are the influencers that, through their activities, have the potential to make decisions or initiate processes that could have a detrimental impact on our operational success.

A good starting point for understanding the political environment in any given country is to start with an analysis of the role these various influencers might play. They can be placed in one of two categories: nonmarket government and nonmarket nongovernment. The former would be both politicians and civil servants. The latter would be opinion leaders and special interest groups.

From a U.S. perspective it would be easy to assume all four of these groups have some influence within a country's political environment but that is not always the case in international markets. Politicians and civil servants are two distinct groups in America. Politicians are elected officials and civil servants are often career professionals whose jobs are not dependent upon the outcome of elections. Gaining the ability to manage the political process means being able to influence those who drive the process. Politicians desire reelection so anything a firm can do that furthers their goal can enable the firm to gain access to them and therefore influence the political process. Civil servants are not directly beholden to the voting public so they are more likely to respond to whatever a firm can do that furthers their relevance or power base within the government bureaucracy.

This difference between the two groups in the nonmarket government environment is clear in the United States but not so well defined in other markets. For example, in China these two groups become one as the country is dominated by a single-party system where the politicians function as civil servants and vice versa. Gaining the attention of these individuals is not about public approval in the electoral process but about holding on to power by controlling any potential public dissonance. The Communist Party in China aims to maintain power through a conscious effort to increase the standard of living—especially in terms of the available and accessible material goods. Outside firms have quickly discovered that as long as they adhere to the government's approach to controlling information flow any material improvements they can provide to Chinese consumers are looked upon favorably by the Chinese government.

In the case of the nonmarket nongovernment side of the political environment there are opinion leaders and special interest groups. An opinion leader would be an individual who draws a substantial number of people to rally around his agenda whether it be civil rights, government reform, or a particular ideology. The groups that gather around these opinion leaders have a tendency to be somewhat homogenous when it comes to personal characteristics such as ethnicity, education, income, geographic location, and so forth. Special interest groups are those that are brought together by a commitment to a specific, narrowly defined agenda such as human rights, gun control, and so forth. The fundamental difference is that a group following an opinion leader is brought together and held together by an individual whereas the special interest groups are brought together by a common cause.

The relevance and power of each of these is predicated upon its ability to reach the general public—in other words, its "voice." This is something that firms can help with as it frequently involves the purchase of media access. But again this assumes that these groups hold some degree of influence in the country. If we consider the example of China once more it is clear that opinion leaders and special interest groups are not important influencers in the political process. We are not suggesting they do not exist—individual dissidents and dissident groups have received a great deal of attention in the global news media. The problem is that they are viewed as engaging in anti-government activities, which means they are outside the law and therefore outside the political process. Theoretically, the political environment can comprise these four groups. Practically, we must carefully consider what really constitutes the "individuals, institutions, and organizations" that make up the political environment.

From there, the next step is to establish the type of environment these individuals and groups operate in. That is, in what context do political activities take place? This discussion could, if taken simply on the face of it, take on the appearance of being an exercise in political science. But it is important that we stay focused on our purpose, which is to have a clear understanding of the political aspects of the market in which we seek to excel. Remember that the political environment dictates the final structure of the rules by which business is conducted in any market so we must pay close attention to that process and any similarities or differences that exist between that market and markets in which we have operational experience.

THE MARKETPLACE AS A NATION-STATE

Placing this political environment into a meaningful context means gaining an understanding of the selected market in terms of it being a "nation-state." It is fair to assume from the perspective of international business that any given country is synonymous with a market. In international business we rightly view country boundaries as the clear delineators of market boundaries. This approach is appropriate largely because of the characteristics of what political scientists would refer to as a nation-state, or what we would refer to as a country, and how authority is exerted in that country.

There are three basic characteristics that define all nation-states or countries. First, a country must have a clearly defined geographic territory. This has several important ramifications for us as businesspeople. It means that this defined geographic territory establishes a finite market space for our business operations. This is important as it helps to focus our efforts in understanding other markets as well as organizing the global marketplace. Further, this defined geographic territory establishes exactly where the political environment we intend to analyze is valid. Finally, recognizing that there are multiple political environments means that our strategic plans, and the implementation of those plans, will be more effective as we tailor our approach to the political environment unique to each market.

A country is also characterized by its sovereignty—or its ability to exercise supreme legal authority within its own borders. What this means for us is that the political process is ultimately backed up by the ability of government officials within that country to enforce, through the legal system, the laws, rules, and regulations that are the result of the political process. In order for a country to exist as a functioning political entity this sovereignty must exist both internally and externally. Internal sovereignty means that ultimate authority to rule is held by those that constitute the government segment of the political environment. If that authority to rule does not exist then a functioning nation-state does not exist and, by extension, a functioning market does not exist. Our goal is to be successful in our international operations. Anarchy is not a defining characteristic we seek out in any market.

External sovereignty, on the other hand, means that other countries recognize and accept another country's internal sovereignty. This means that other countries accept the legitimacy of the political and legal structure in the market in question. This is not just a theoretical issue in political science—it has profound implications for us as businesspeople. The existence of external sovereignty helps us to have a certain level of confidence in the stability of that market. Put another way, if other countries accept the political structure that exists in a given country as the legitimate rule of law there is much less likelihood that the status quo in this market will be threatened—it will be more stable over the long term.

An example of the importance of having a firm understanding of the legitimacy of both the internal and external sovereignty of a market would be Iraq. Prior to the recent conflict, Iraq was viewed by many firms—French in particular—as being a stable, attractive market. Their assessment was heavily skewed toward their analysis of the political environment from the viewpoint of internal sovereignty. It would be hard to argue that Iraq at the time was not characterized by a strong internal sovereignty. Saddam Hussein, and his Bath Party, had unquestioned ultimate rule within the country's borders. From the perspective of French firms, this meant that any deal struck with the government—and there were several very large deals involving oil rights—would be upheld without question or debate. Unfortunately for those firms, the deals that were concluded were predicated not only on the stability of Iraq's internal sovereignty but also its external sovereignty. When the U.S.-led coalition determined that Saddam's government no longer was a good global citizen and had forfeited the right to exercise rule-of-law in the country, the invasion occurred with the subsequent change in the political environment and, ultimately, French firms seeing their previously concluded deals being forfeited.

The last characteristic of a country is the existence of monopoly power. Put simply, this means that the existing political system, and the legal structure that is the product of the political process, has the sole right and authority to exercise unquestioned power in that country. For us this means that the existing government has, in the end, the last word in enforcement of the laws, rules, and regulations that control business activities.

From a U.S. point of view this might be considered to be a potential threat—we tend to prefer operating with a minimal level of government interference. However, the existence of a clearly established and controlled market can have its advantages especially if we are new to that market or to international operations in general. We prefer an absence of government activity in our home market because we are intimately familiar with that market. Moving into a new market means that uncertainty is increased, which makes decision making problematic. The presence of a strong political system means that a certain amount of uncertainty has been reduced, which should make it easier for us to make good, lasting decisions in that market. What form then does this "monopoly power" take? This leads us to the issue of how authority is exerted within a country—or in other words, the nature of the political environment.

SOURCES OF AUTHORITY IN A NATION-STATE

In the current global economy there are five different types of government that are universally recognized as legitimate means of exercising authority within a country. These are considered recognized in that they are viewed as possessing internal and external sovereignty by the majority of other nations that compose the world economy. Each exercises control differently, and the composition of the political environment in terms of the active players— government and nongovernment—can vary as all might be present and exert power or some, as discussed previously, may be absent. For the sake of our discussion, one specific type of political system is omitted. That is the dictatorship. Recent history has shown, not only in the case of Iraq but around the world, that in the increasingly intertwined global economy, the external sovereignty of these dictatorships is being called into question with the result being that they are generally viewed as unstable business environments.

If we exclude a dictator-state as a legitimate political environment in which to operate we are left with five different alternatives. The first of these would be a traditional monarchy, such as Saudi Arabia, where absolute sovereignty is vested in a hereditary ruler. At this point it would be appropriate to ask how a traditional monarchy, where power is wielded by a single individual or family, differs from a dictatorship. The answer is simple: a traditional monarchy is recognized as a legitimate political system by other countries. It enjoys that vital characteristic of external sovereignty that for us equates to political stability, something lacking in a dictatorship. Therefore, provided our firm's means of operation and product offering are approved by the powers that be in the traditional monarchy, this type of political structure can be especially appealing.

The second type of political system would be the constitutional monarchy—the most notable example being Great Britain. We can view the constitutional monarchy as a hybrid where elements exist of the traditional monarchy and our system in the United States—the constitutional republic. In a constitutional monarchy a hereditary monarch exists as the head of state, but government functions are performed through elected democratic institutions. For example, in Great Britain, the Queen is considered the head of the government and the Prime Minister, and their accompanying government, serves at her pleasure. The political process operates through elected officials but in the event that there is a lack of public confidence in this elected government elections can be called at any time—not on a strictly established schedule like the United States. This injects a certain amount of uncertainty in government policies as priorities can shift dramatically in s short period of time. At the same time, the constitutional monarchy is considered to be an attractive political environment for business due to its democratic foundation—one where the political environment is created and maintained through a deliberate, transparent process.

Here it is important to note the role of the monarch in the constitutional monarchy. Too often it is assumed that the monarch strictly serves the role of a ceremonial figurehead. That is too superficial a conclusion. It is true that the monarch—using Great Britain as an example—has no overt role in the political process. Laws and regulations are created and passed without her direct involvement. However, it would be shortsighted to conclude the monarch plays no role at all. On a higher level, the monarch sets the tone for the long-term direction of the country. She accomplishes this through her personification of the country's national identity—a concept whose importance we will discuss in the next chapter. Those of us who come from a constitutional republic can easily downplay the importance of the monarch in a constitutional monarchy but a conversation with any citizen of such a country will quickly dispel the myth that the monarch is only a figurehead.

Thus our discussion turns to the third type of political system, the constitutional republic. In a constitutional republic sovereignty is codified in a basic document—most commonly a constitution—and the various laws and regulations are built around this foundation. Most countries considered active and developed economies, such as the United States, Germany, France, Mexico, are constitutional republics.

A constitutional republic is often the favored type of market environment for firms to enter because of the relative open and transparent means by which the political process, and subsequent legal environment, functions. In addition, the political cycle—specifically the electoral cycle—is predetermined. Just as we know exactly when elections are scheduled in the United States (and the resulting potential for changes in the political environment) we can anticipate the timing of potential changes that greatly reduces uncertainty in the environment. This being said, it makes changes in the political environment easier to anticipate. It does not eliminate uncertainty. Change in the political environment of a constitutional republic, from a business perspective, can be significant—the difference between this type of political system and others being that the so-called change points are established through the scheduled elections. A constitutional republic is not necessarily more stable over time; the points at which change might occur are just more predictable.

The last two types of political systems could, from the perspective of U.S. firms, be considered special cases. These are the theocracy/quasi-theocracy and the Communist state. In the former, power is exercised by either the head of a particular religion or through a religious group. At true theocracy is a political system that exists solely based on a particular religion; that is, there are no other political or governmental systems. Afghanistan during the rule of the Taliban would be an example of a theocracy. From a more practical standpoint, most countries where religions play an important role in defining the political environment exist as quasi-theocracies (e.g., Iran). In such a country, religion plays a central role in defining the political environment but other political structures, like a parliament with opposition parties, also exists. This typically means that the political environment is directed by the predominant religious belief system. However, the speed of change in the environment is tempered by a certain level of debate and discourse. The key to success in this type of political environment is to ensure your firm's operations and product offerings do not run afoul of the norms and values of the religion.

The final type of political system that might come into play would be a Communist state. Currently there is only one viable market in the global economy that is Communist, but it is a significant player—China. In the Chinese Communist system, sovereignty rests with the party and is exercised through a core of strong leaders. This means that in China's unique political environment the government influencers—politicians and civil servants—hold power and the nongovernment influencers—opinion leaders and special interest groups—are outside of the political process. The high level of government involvement in the economy becomes a two-edged sword. On the one hand, the government's close control over all aspects of life injects a certain level of certainty into operations. At the same time, without the checks and balances that firms from developed economies are used to, there can be diminished opportunities as the government seeks to limit the amount of influence outside firms have within China.

THE POLITICAL ENVIRONMENT
AND INTERNATIONAL BUSINESS

All of this political discussion is a very necessary initial step in conducting an assessment of the political environment in a country. It is impossible to fully understand the types of threats that must be dealt with if there is no clear understanding of the type of political system that operates in the country. But we need to continue to move toward applying this knowledge in a practical sense. That means our discussion must now move toward focusing on the specific characteristics of the political environment that might be considered red flags, the ways these red flags might manifest themselves as real threats to our business, and what can be done to manage these threats.

In identifying the likelihood that there may be the potential for political threats to our operations in a given country the best place to start is with the form and degree to which the government is involved in market activity. We would need to consider the extent to which the government is directly involved in the market through such activities as provided goods and services (i.e., a welfare state), how involved the government is in economic development—either directly through government-sponsored programs or indirectly through government support to local firms (e.g., protectionist trade barriers), and the means by which the government controls the economy (i.e., through fiscal or monetary policies).

When the government is heavily involved in provided goods and services it could be considered to be a competitor—depending upon how those goods and services relate to your firm and its product offering. When this occurs, firms sometimes panic unnecessarily because they assume that the government will always have the upper hand in any competitive confrontation. It is true that governments often do have a competitive advantage given that they control business activities. However, experience has shown that while governments may have critical mass that does not always translate into competitive advantage. Governments are in the business of governing—not in business. This tends to mean they are inefficient and those inefficiencies lead to opportunities. Take the example of the health care system in Britain. The government provides health care to all legal residents through the National Health Service (NHS). Yet there is a thriving system of private doctors, hospital, and clinics. Where the government has to be all things to all people, private physicians and clinics can specialize resulting in a higher standard— or a perceived higher standard—of care to patients. Similarly, when the government becomes involved in economic development programs—regardless of whether this is direct or indirect involvement—there tends to be a lack of efficiency when compared to the efforts of private firms, which also opens up opportunity.

The means by which the government controls the economy also becomes an important issue. Typically, control of an economy is exercised either through monetary policy, fiscal policy, or some combination thereof. In the case of the former the ramifications for international firms can often be a restriction in the firm's ability to achieve maximum profitability. Controlling the money supply through interest rates, currency rules, and exchange regulations may have the desired effect from the perspective of the economy in the country in question but these may have serious negative consequences for the profits of an outside firm. In the case of fiscal policy, where economic control is heavily influenced by tax policy, the obvious and easy target of tax increases is always outside firms. Either way, if the government has active and ongoing monetary and/or fiscal policy programs the potential for your profitability to be negatively impacted is very real.

There are some other aspects of the political environment, beyond direct government involvement in the economy, which could signal problems for international firms that we must also consider. For example, how aggressive is the government in enforcing the laws it has on the books that would help to protect your firm. China has all the laws and regulations a firm might expect when it comes to protecting intellectual property—the problem is that the Chinese government has a poor track record of enforcement. Another area to consider is the extent to which the government monitors the environmental impact of a firm's operations and products. This could go beyond just the traditional environmental issues such as pollution and extend to the impact on society—such as public health issues (e.g., the negative aspects of fast food). There is also the potential problems associated with layers—national, state, local—of the political environment. There is not always a simple set of rules for operations that apply universally in a market. Imported beer firms operating in the United States have to deal with not only the universal drinking age, but also state statutes governing the form the product takes and where it can be sold (states in the Midwest only allow beer with a limited alcohol content to be sold outside of liquor stores), as well as local laws governing when the product can be sold (e.g., time of day and day of the week).

WHEN FIRMS AND GOVERNMENTS COLLIDE

We are beginning to get a more focused picture regarding what specifically to look for when it comes to identifying potential threats in the political environment. It would now be helpful to think more closely about how those threats would manifest themselves to a firm. In other words, what is the result of a collision between firms and a government?

Firms and governments collide—usually with negative results for the firm—when governments, or the political entities that constitute a government or political system, feel threatened. Sometimes this threat is viewed by the government in question as a direct threat to its sovereignty. Obviously it would be pretty unusual for a company to want to get directly involved in governing a country. However, it may be that through the normal course of doing business the firm's activities do represent a direct threat to the government's ongoing ability to exercise authority in its own country. We have to look no further than China and the restrictions that are placed on technology and information transfer à la Google. Google has no desire to exercise authority in China, but the company's product—information transfer—is viewed as a direct threat by the Chinese government given that one of the prime means by which the Communist Party maintains power is through the control of information flow.

A second way that firms and the political environment can collide would be when political conflict is created. This is a situation where the firm becomes somehow involved in conflict between entities—government and/or nongovernment—that make up the political environment. For example, a firm's operations may draw it into controversy in the political environment. In the 1990s, McDonald's became a target for radical elements in the agricultural sector in France largely because the restaurants were viewed as an outside force for cultural change. Individual consumers had little problem with the firm—as evidenced by sales—but some in the agricultural sector considered McDonald's to be a negative influence encouraging the consumption of "non-French" food.

Alternatively, political threats can be the result of conflict between the firm's home and host governments. When countries come into conflict, it is not uncommon for that conflict to be played out in the arena of international business. Over the years, the U.S. and Japanese governments have used firms and industries as their weapons in establishing trade rules between the two markets. The United States has, in the past, threatened tariffs on the key industries upon which the Japanese export economy relies (e.g., automobiles) in order to coerce the Japanese to open up unrelated areas of their market such as agricultural products. This has nothing to do with the activities of the industry, or the firms that make up that industry, it is simply a situation where the firms and their products represent an easy target to further the agenda of those in the political environment.

This collision results in one of three types of political threats. The first type is generally referred to as an equity and management threat. These are targeted at who controls the firm. The most common forms would include some degree of nationalization, a forced joint venture, or restrictions on the number of foreign managers. All these would have the same result—decision making in the firm would reside either directly or indirectly with the host government not with the firm. The second type, known as earnings and performance threats, is targeted not at decision making within the firm but at control of the profits. Common earnings and performance threats would be currency exchange controls and revenue repatriation controls. The third type would be operational threats (e.g., product content laws, price ceilings and floors, distribution restrictions) that would restrict the means by which the firm can implement its business model.

ASSESSING POLITICAL VULNERABILITY

So, how can we come to some determination as to the extent of our possible political vulnerability in another country? In order to make this assessment we need to look internally at firm-specific issues that could open your firm up to political threats and externally at the market-specific issues that are associated with political vulnerability. The internal, firm-specific issues are those that are unique to the firm. The external, market-specific issues are those that could be a sign of political vulnerability for firms entering that market regardless of industry or product type.

In assessing political vulnerability from an internal perspective we need to look directly at the firm's product offering and its potential impact within the market under consideration. One question to ask would be does the firm and its product encourage political debates? The original abortion pill (known as RU-486) was introduced into the U.S. market several years ago by a French firm. This firm greatly underestimated the power of the debate between pro-life and pro-choice factions in the U.S. political environment. As a result, the adoption and diffusion of the product in the U.S. market was greatly hampered. Firms are also more politically vulnerable if their operations somehow involve media and mass communication. This could be because of the product offering (e.g., Google in China) or the indirect result of the company's business model (e.g., the use of mass communication through advertising). Other firm-specific characteristics that are associated with political vulnerability would be a negative impact on local firms, a situation where your company's product offering has a large service component, or where your product offering is potentially hazardous—either through potential physical harm to a user or social harm to the society at large.

Trying to come to grips with the external or market-specific issues that might represent political vulnerability for your firm involves trying to identify potential problems that all firms entering this market may face. The best place to start would be to revisit the type of political or government structure that exists in the market (see previous discussion). Our main concern is to gain some understanding as to the type of government so we have a clear picture of how the political process operates and also to assess the stability of the government/political system. Understanding the former places us in a better spot for determining the form any political threats may take while the latter is of the utmost importance to us—firms want to avoid markets where the political environment is unstable as such an environment would have a high level of uncertainty.

Moving beyond the type and stability of the government and associated political environment we then consider the role the government plays in the marketplace. As we have previously discussed, governments can be involved in an economy as a facilitator or as a provider. From a political perspective, the facilitator role typically doesn't mean that the government eliminates political barriers in order to facilitate economic activity; rather, a facilitating role would more likely mean that the government—through the political process—has established and enforced laws and regulations governing the conduct of business. This clear set of objective rules serves to facilitate market activities as those involved have a transparent view of how business can, and cannot, be conducted. This reduces uncertainty for outside firms and is typically viewed as a positive situation.

On the other hand, when the government plays the provider role it means that the government has the potential to be an active competitor depending upon the sector or industry in which the government is active. If your firm's product offering overlaps with a given government's role as provider in its market this represents a potentially serious political threat. In direct competition a government will more than likely have advantages over a company from the outside. The best way to minimize this vulnerability would be to look for any possible niche opportunities that may be created through government inefficiencies in its market operations. In most cases governments are involved in a particular industry as a service to society. This means that moving to a more specialized area within a given industry is not viewed as a competitive threat by the government—and may enable you and your firm to enjoy the revenue benefits of offering a premium-priced product.

CONDUCTING AN ASSESSMENT OF THE POLITICAL ENVIRONMENT

The political environment is incredibly complex and being able to understand the complexities of any given market environment is key to the likelihood we will be successful in our efforts in that market. In order to accomplish this analysis effectively we must answer the following questions/issues.

What Is the Nature of the Political Environment?

- Who are the relevant players in the country (government vs. nongovernment)?
- Does the country exhibit all the characteristics of a functional nation-state?
- By what means is power exerted in the country (traditional monarchy, constitutional monarchy, theocracy/quasi-theocracy, constitutional republic, or Communist state)?

Specific Aspects of the Political Environment

- Extent to which a welfare state exists
- Regional development policies
- Use of fiscal vs. monetary policy
- Environmental policies
- Government enforcement of laws and regulations pertaining to business
- Extent to which power/authority is divided (e.g., national vs. regional vs. local)

Business-Government Interaction

- Does your firm and its activities represent a potential sovereignty threat?
- Does your firm and its activities have the potential to create political conflict?
- To what extent might equity and management threats (who controls the firm) be a problem?
- To what extent might earnings and performance threats (who profits from the firm) be a problem?
- To what extent might operational threats (how the firm operates) be a problem?

Assessing Political Vulnerability (Firm-Specific Issues)

- Is the firm or its products potentially involved in political debates?
- Is the firm involved in mass communication (directly or indirectly)?

- What is the potential effect of firm operations on local businesses?
- Is your product offering a service, or does it have a large service component?
- Is your product offering potentially hazardous (to individuals or society as a whole)?

SUMMARY

In this chapter we first made a distinction between the political and legal environment. Because the political environment involves the process by which the legal environment is created we focused on understanding how that process might work in a given market as well as what firms can do to influence the process. Defining the political environment as being outside of the normal transactional environment usually associated with international business, we considered the different groups that make up the political environment, how they think, and what firms can do in order to manage each group. The discussion then turned to the different types of market nation-states, the sources of authority in these nation-states, and what each might mean for businesses operating within each type. The latter part of the chapter involved a discussion of how the political environment can specifically impact operational aspects of international business and both the sources of, and management tactics for, political risk. Finally, a framework for conducting an assessment of the political environment was presented.

4

The Social Imperative: Culture and Cultural Differences

INTRODUCTION

When we look at the social imperative we must understand that we are essentially looking at culture. Culture can be a tricky discussion in international business. It is very easy for the terms *international* and *cultural differences* to become somewhat interchangeable. If we were to ask a group of businesspeople what makes international business unique the response from many would be cultural differences. It should be abundantly clear by now that there is much, much more to international business than just dealing with cultural differences. Further, depending upon your company's area of operation and product offering, cultural differences may be irrelevant. Having said this, understanding the social imperative as it relates to culture is still an important piece of the puzzle if we are to have an accurate picture of the market in which we are considering operations. This means we need to consider culture from the perspective of international business.

Studying the social imperative, or environment, involves the study of human interaction—and the foundation of human interaction is culture. Over the years in the area of international business, culture has been defined differently. The first accepted definition was "the man-made part of the human environment."[1] This was then expanded by Geert Hofstede to "the collective programming of the mind which distinguishes the members of one human group from another."[2] More recently culture was defined as "all learned behavior shared by a society."[3] Given that we are not sociologists, what practical use do any of these definitions have for us as businesspeople? The answer is that they all provide some practical knowledge of what is important to us about culture. All three of these definitions show us that culture is *learned*, it is *shared*, and it is *enforced*.

Why are these characteristics so important? Because it helps us to move beyond the mindset that different cultures mean we are faced with differences we can't control and must, therefore, adapt to. This "differences" mindset also tends to propagate the myth that cultural differences are automatically important to our business efforts. This mindset is simply unproductive in terms of our desire to successfully operate in another market. So what *can* we get from the fact that culture is learned, shared, and enforced? Let's consider what culture is, and what culture is not.

WHAT IS "CULTURE"?

We will start with what culture is. First, culture is learned. No one emerges from the womb possessing the characteristics of a particular culture. Whether we want to characterize culture as "learned behavior," "collective programming," or just values and beliefs everyone learns how to act within the culture in which they exist. Where do these lessons come from? Obviously from our parents and family members, but also from other sources. As people around the world become increasingly part of the global information explosion—via the Internet, smart phones, and other forms of technology—we are getting our lessons of how to act in order to fit into society from nontraditional sources. The bottom line is that culture is learned, so it can be taught—and those lessons can be taught by companies in the form of advertising, social media, really any message we choose to send. As a company we can also tie our firm and its products to existing cultural values. For example, in a market where the culture places a high value on the environment we could associate our products with this value set by emphasizing the recyclability of the package. Either way, the first lesson we need to take on board is that culture is learned, which means we, as a business, can become involved in that learning process rather than just resigning ourselves to the notion that we must fully understand a culture so we can adapt to it.

Second, culture is shared. Culture represents a set of values, and the resulting behaviors, not of individuals, but which the collective population accepts. If we were to set out to segment a market it would be easy to identify truly unique characteristics of individuals that we could effectively target. However, it would not be remotely efficient to build any business model around individuals. What we seek is characteristics that are shared by large groups of individuals. That is exactly what culture represents. Within any given culture there might be vast differences between individuals over a wide range of beliefs—such as religious affiliations in the United States. At the same time, however, American culture has shared values that influence how we behave—such as the importance of personal rights and freedom. Just as culture should not be viewed as an unmanageable threat if we take into account the fact that it can be taught we should also see the positive side of culture for our business activities—the values and beliefs that bind a culture together create for us actionable market segments.

Third, and finally, culture is enforced. Obviously we don't generally take this literally—although some countries such as Iran do actively enforce cultural norms through organizations such as the religious police. More typically, cultural norms are enforced by the society that adopts these beliefs. Humans are interactive creatures—we all need to feel we belong to a group. In order to be a member of a group we need to adhere to the rules of that group, or society. Failure to do so will result in our being sanctioned by the group, or even cast out of the group. The validation of cultural beliefs and values comes in their representing the rules that establish the group we, as humans, all seek to belong to. They are enforced simply because they serve as the structure for the group. Thus, if in our business endeavors we are able to credibly associate our company and its products with these accepted cultural norms we can have confidence that our customers in that market will not readily reject our offering as it would go against that which they seek to be associated with.

We have established what culture is, and by extension what it is not. Culture is not inherited; it is learned over time and is dynamic rather than static. Understanding a culture is also not about understanding individual values; we are looking for macro characteristics that draw individuals together not micro characteristics that identify them as individuals. The focus is on similarities not differences. There is one last characteristic that we must also accept before we can go any further in terms of being able to practically and effectively operate in another culture. Identifying cultural characteristics, or differences between cultures, is not about right and wrong.

If we are not careful, it is easy to fall into the trap of judging other cultures from the vantage point of our own. Using your own cultural values to make value determinations about another culture is commonly referred to as the application of a self-reference criterion. When we do this we are using our own value set as a filter to draw conclusions about what is right and what is wrong when it comes to another culture. While this might be an appropriate exercise for us to engage in as individuals we must not lose sight of the part we are playing as business decision makers. Our goal is not to determine which cultures are most like our own—our goal is to use our knowledge of another culture in order to effectively operate in that culture. We must be objectively focused on what cultural differences might mean to our business potential and how best to deal with those differences not subjectively focused on whether or not we approve of a culture's value set.

THE INGREDIENTS OF CULTURE

Coming to terms with the idea of culture, along with its attendant values and beliefs, helps us to understand what culture is and isn't in the context of international business. But the concepts of *values* and *beliefs* are very big indeed. In order to be able to come to grips with these large constructs it is most helpful for us to think about what these various values and beliefs might be associated with. In other words, can they somehow be organized so that we have a more useful understanding of how the cultural environment in one country might differ from, or alternatively be similar to, that of our home market? These so-called ingredients of culture can be divided into one of five distinct categories: material culture, social culture, the natural world, aesthetics, and language.

A good place for us to begin would be to consider material culture—given its importance in the American value system. Material culture refers to values and meanings related to the tangible. A culture, like the United States, that places a high emphasis on material products is one in which members of that culture define and describe themselves based on their consumption. In other words, we are what we have. For anyone who has lived in America it would be difficult to argue the importance we place on our "stuff." The proliferation of brand names, the wide range of product choices, even our high debt limits all signal a great deal of emphasis being placed on consumption.

For companies, domestic and nondomestic, this particular characteristic of the U.S. culture is a real advantage. In a material culture it is relatively easy to market a product as consumers are already actively seeking out more, different, and better goods and services. This means the cultural "lessons" we provide (i.e., that consuming our product will help fulfill their material culture needs) is unlikely to meet resistance; on the contrary it is a message that solidly fits into that culture. How do we know if a culture places a high level of importance on the material aspect? By observing the extent to which products play a visible and positive role in that culture.

In contrast, a culture that places a high level of importance on social culture is one where the values and meanings related to intangible, human-to-human interactions take precedent. In a social culture, members are not defined by their material wealth but by their relationships. Simple observations of individuals in the United States show us the contrast between a material and a social culture. Listen to the conversations at a cocktail party. Two people engage in a conversation. One goes on for several minutes about his new car/new job/vacation/favorite restaurant/virtually any consumption experience. He pauses and the second person launches into almost an identical list of her consumptive accomplishments. Neither takes much notice of the other, in fact no real communication—as measured by an exchange of ideas—has occurred.

In a social culture members not only engage in interactions where the focus is on the interaction but they seek out opportunities to engage in meaningful social discourse. Where a material culture is tailor-made for businesses, a social culture is much more challenging. Rather than encouraging consumption for consumption's sake, the firm and its product must now credibly demonstrate that what it has to offer has some sort of social value. While this may be a challenge it is not impossible if we are willing to look beyond the more familiar aspects of products. It is relatively easy to convince people in a material culture of the desirability of an expensive car simply based on the premium brand name. Where a social culture might not respond to an overt appeal to materialism, it may be quite credible to introduce a buying proposal for the same car built around the quality = safety premise and/or quality = longevity (i.e., responsible use of financial resources). This very appeal has been used over the years by Mercedes Benz in markets where it has been determined that the social elements of culture play an important role.

The third category of values is the natural world. This takes into account human-spiritual interactions. While this area could cross into a discussion of "man" and "God," we are consciously avoiding the terms *religion* and *religious* for a couple of reasons. One would be that any discussion of humans' relationship with the natural world could easily degenerate into a discussion/argument of spiritual right and wrong. There is no value in this type of discussion in international business. A second good reason for avoiding the terms *religion* and *religious* is that they are not always accurate in providing a meaningful description of another culture. Consider what we mean when we say that an individual, or group of individuals, are "religious." In most cases, we are referring to how openly they practice a set of religious beliefs and/or are openly associated with those beliefs. We are generally not referring to whether or not different thought patterns or behaviors are the result of this religiosity.

For our purposes, as businesspeople trying to come to grips with another culture, how often individuals in a culture attend the mosque, synagogue, church, temple, or shrine is not really relevant unless our product offering is directly related to those activities. We are more concerned with how a belief system that addresses the relationship between humans and their greater existence might influence the way they behave in the marketplace. In so-called Western cultures the belief system in this area tends to be vertical in nature. That is, humans are at the top of a natural hierarchy. This means the world around us exists for our pleasure (i.e., we control the world around us) and this attitude is reflected in our behaviors as consumers—many of the products we buy are for our own pleasure and the effect of our consumption does not enter into our consciousness. In other words, a material-focused culture. Other cultures, such as those dominated by Islam, Hinduism, and Buddhism, are more horizontal in make-up, which means human existence is in parallel with the world around us causing the resulting culture to take on more social characteristics relative to consumption.

How is this different from the categories of material and social culture? Understanding values centered around the human–natural world relationship gives us an insight into the foundation of the culture—the other aspects typically are the result of the foundational values surrounding the human-natural world relationship and these values are less changeable over time. For example, few would argue the statement "America is not a religious country." Measured by worship attendance that is probably a fairly accurate statement. However, our cultural foundation is firmly rooted in "religious" principles. Namely, the concept of individual rights and freedoms upon which the U.S. Constitution is based—which, in turn, was based on the Puritan concept of individual salvation. Our culture is strongly influenced by values related to humans and the natural world. As Americans we generally don't see this because we can't see beyond the concept of "religion."

The last two ingredients of culture—aesthetics and language—are closely related. Both involve the transfer of ideas—communication—through our senses. Aesthetics is about the transfer of values and meanings through visual communications where language is about the transfer of these same values and ideas through verbal communications. Neither are as clearly defined, or quite as easy to describe, as the first three ingredients of culture but they are important nonetheless. In the case of the former, aesthetics, we may not be able to specifically describe these values but we know when those norms have been violated. It has been shown that consumers in a culture will attach negative associations to commercial communications such as an advertisement because it looks "funny" or "foreign."

Mentos candy advertisements in the United States have, in the past, been considered by American consumers to possess a "foreign" look. Were we to storyboard these ads they probably wouldn't look substantially different from the ads of other similar products. But the way in which they are presented visually causes U.S. consumers to see them as "foreign" and by extension not only feel uncomfortable with the way the product is being presented but also, potentially, with the product itself. In a similar vein, nonnative language either in the form of the actual language used or in the phrases and accents that are heard can cause the listener to feel uncomfortable with the way the communication is presented and therefore quite possibly the content of the message as well.

Although the aesthetic aspects of culture may be difficult to decipher, language can tell us a great deal about a culture. Language is the means by which individuals communicate—by necessity the way in which we describe our interactions with people along with how we describe our relationship with the greater world around us. We don't have to be fluent in any given language to pick up the lessons it can provide us about a culture. Understanding how a language constructs meanings that can be used to effectively communicate between individuals and groups of individuals is a powerful tool for understanding different cultures. One of the most heavily used words in American English is the word *I*—a very clear indication of how people who identify with American culture tend to focus on themselves. In contrast, the absence of this same type of phraseology in the Japanese culture—the fact that it is impolite to refer directly to one's self in conversation—is a clear indication that for the Japanese culture at least it's not "all about me."

CULTURE AND INTERNATIONAL BUSINESS: INTERNAL ORGANIZATIONAL CHALLENGES

Culture can affect international business in two basic areas. First, culture can create internal organizational challenges particularly when it comes to managing employees with different cultural values. Cultural differences can also create external challenges for a firm's market activities.

When there is a clear difference between the value system of the home country and the firm's employees in the host market there is a potential for value conflicts or, at the very least, the potential for different interpretations. This can make communication difficult and result in a dysfunctional work environment. Oftentimes the product of these conflicts, in addition to the possibility of polarizing different groups of employees, is the creation of ethical issues. A more traditional culture where a gender hierarchy exists could be an environment in which sexual harassment becomes problematic as these cultures often accept the notion that females are somehow inferior to males. While this attitude may be acceptable to local inhabitants it would be unacceptable in the United States. This raises the question: do we manage our business in the host market along the lines of local cultural values or do we ensure fair and unbiased treatment of employees of both genders, at least within our firm? Not an easy question to answer and this is just one possible scenario that might arise when cultural values conflict.

Another typical internal conflict point relates to the motivational tools available to managers—especially in different cultural concepts of reward. Firms and managers from the United States, indeed from many of the Western cultures, tend to focus their managerial motivation techniques on extrinsic rewards; that is, rewards that represent some form of tangible benefit (i.e., monetary bonuses, wage increases, etc.). In a material-based culture an extrinsic reward system is well suited to values related to acquiring, or having the ability to acquire, more material goods and services. By singling individual employees out with extrinsic rewards such a system is also consistent with the individually centered competitive employment environment associated with material cultures.

But what if your firm operates in a culture where your employees have a value system grounded in cultural values that do not easily fit the extrinsic/material-oriented cultural model (e.g. a social-oriented culture)? In this situation, the manager must seek to build an intrinsic reward system where the focus is on making the employee "feel good" about his role within the company. This system would need to address two facets of intrinsic rewards: the need to build up the employee without drawing undo attention to him within the organization and tie any overt reward(s) to his value to the firm and other members of his team, not to his individual accomplishments. The intrinsic reward system centers on rewarding the employee's contribution to the firm (i.e., "social" group) not on his ability to generate material benefits for himself outside of the firm.

Taking into account the myriad of potential problems that a firm and its managers might face in dealing with employees—and managers—from different cultures, many firms take a proactive stance and try to devise an organizational environment that supersedes cultural differences. One method of accomplishing this is the value-based approach. In this approach, the difficulties associated with cultural differences—at least within the firm—are significantly reduced or eliminated through the construction of a strong corporate culture. IBM's recent promotional campaign has been built around the concept of employees as "IBMers." This is a decades-old concept within the firm's corporate culture. When an individual goes to work at IBM—a well-established multinational with employees and sites across the globe— she enters into the corporate culture of IBM. That is, she is indoctrinated in the corporate value system and required—when in her role as employee— to adhere to this corporate value system rather than her individual cultural value system. This is an effective technique for firms of all sizes—it is actually much easier to introduce and manage as the firm gets smaller as it is essentially developing a team-oriented work environment. Beyond the advantage of flexibility in terms of firm size it is also flexible in terms of firm type—it can be effectively used in manufacturing, technology, service, or really any type of business.

Another means of proactively dealing with cultural differences in an organization is the process-based approach. The organization that adopts a process-based approach strives to develop a common technical or professional culture within the firm. Where the value-based approach is flexible when it comes to the type of company in which it can be effective, the process-based approach is generally only effective in companies where the employee activities are all focused on a singular goal—such as manufacturing a product. Goodyear Tire and Rubber has employees and facilities around the world but its focus is pretty narrow—the manufacture and sale of tires. Every employee, regardless of her location or home culture, knows exactly what her role is in the company whether it is product design, product manufacture, or product sale. Goodyear's experience has shown that this approach is very effective in bridging cultural gaps, sometimes even helping to overcome language barriers, within the company.

The dependency-approach is less subtle, but effective under certain well-defined circumstances. When operations across a variety of cultures must be effectively managed in a short period of time it is possible to apply this authoritarian approach. Under a dependency-approach the firm is centrally controlled through the power of strong financial and planning systems. It is essentially the creation of an organizational dictatorship. This can produce quick results when it comes to dealing with cultural conflicts within an organization but its success is completely based on the ability of those with the central control to apply the use of power. It doesn't engender any level of organizational loyalty, as was the case with the value- and process-based approaches, but it is a fast means of addressing the problem.

Last is the organizational approach that ignores cultural differences. In almost every circumstance it is not a good course of action in business—domestic or international—to ignore a problem. However, in the case of cultural differences, a case can be made—in certain situations—where ignoring cultural differences is the best way for an organization to effectively deal with them. It may be that the cultural differences that exist do not represent a problem to the organization. Firms with dispersed authority and compartmentalized areas of responsibility may find that cultural differences exist within the organization as a whole but there is not significant overlap or interaction between employees of different cultures. In this scenario it is likely in everyone's best interest to leave well enough alone. It is equally conceivable that something other than a corporate-wide approach would be more effective. Ignoring cultural differences—at least when it comes to managing employees from a variety of cultures—is the approach large fast food franchises such as McDonald's choose to adopt. They are very involved in managing their franchisees when it comes to menu offering, quality control, facility placement and management, pricing, promotion and advertising, and so forth. At the same time, they recognize that those most well equipped to manage local employees are the local restaurant owners and managers. The strength of the parent firm is in the business model, not in local employee knowledge. It makes little sense for the parent firm to dictate how to manage employees in a large number of different cultures when the local owners and managers come from these cultures. So, the case is made to simply ignore the cultural differences, at least at the overall organizational level.

CULTURE AND MARKET ACTIVITIES: IMPACT ON STRATEGY

Externally, culture impact on strategy is most evident in its effect on market activities. A constructive means of trying to organize and evaluate where culture and market activities may require action on the part of the firm is by putting these market activities into the context of the 4Ps of marketing. Every aspect of market activities—product, promotion, distribution (physical movement), and price—has the potential to be influenced by cultural differences.

A product represents the value offering of a firm. It is more than just a good or service—it is the entire value bundle that a customer receives in the course of his transactions with a firm. Culture can conceivably cause a company to change the actual physical product itself in order to provide these underlying values. Mattel has discovered over the years that Barbie dolls must be changing physically in order to remain relevant in other cultures. In some Asian cultures Barbie's proportions—height and bust size in particular—are modified in order to better match the physical attributes of females in those markets. Interestingly, Mattel does not alter Barbie's facial characteristics—leaving her a Caucasian. The logic behind this decision, based on extensive market research, is that the value in the doll is that it represents an idealized mechanism for role-playing and females in these markets have a positive view of Caucasian features. Similarly, in more traditional markets it is not the Barbie doll itself that requires change but the product line. This may mean a de-emphasis on Barbie's accoutrements—cars, houses, planes—and a focus on other more realistic and less excessively materialistic items like clothes.

Other changes to the product offering would go beyond the product(s) itself and the organization of the product line. These changes might include the means by which the product is presented—using crockery when selling coffee rather than paper cups in order to support the premium-product positioning strategy—or a change in the product package—adjusting the size to match the storage and product use behavior of the consumers in that market. In all cases, changes to a product strategy are driven by the need to ensure the product represents a meaningful bundle of values to consumers who have a different set of cultural values and, perhaps, can only experience the product's value if it reflects those cultural values.

Promotion, communicating with the market regarding your product, or value offering, can be directly impacted by cultural differences simply by virtue of the fact that communication across cultures represents a serious challenge. Further, these problems go well beyond just those associated with language and translation issues. That is not to discount these "mechanical" issues—it is crucial that we consider things like whether the brand name used in that market fulfills the requirements of a good brand (at the forefront is the translatability of the brand and the need for the brand to carry some sort of positive connotation related to the product itself) and that the means by which we communicate is culturally acceptable.

These are more or less self-evident. What may not be quite as obvious is the underlying content of the promotional message. The product positioning—the foundation of any promotional communication—must be relevant, credible, and culturally acceptable. Cosmetic firms find that positioning their products as "make-up"—something that makes the user more attractive—is acceptable in some markets but too direct a positioning strategy in other cultures. These same products—often without any physical product change—are positioned as "skin care" products in more conservative or traditional cultures. A subtle but important change. Along these same lines, the interactions used in the promotions—that is, individuals using the product—must also be altered. A mouthwash promotion may show two people discussing the virtues of the product—clean breath makes a person more attractive to the opposite sex—in a very direct way in some markets but have to be less direct in others. As was the case with the need to make the product a value bundle that is actually valued by consumers in another market the message you send to those same consumers must be in a form that they are willing to "listen" to and the content of that same message must be of value.

The third of the four Ps is distribution—delivering the value offering. It is a common error to view distribution as only the physical movement of a good, or a logistical problem to be overcome. Distribution does involve the mechanical movement of a product, but its basic purpose is to not only to make the product accessible to your consumers but also to establish and maintain contact with those consumers. This means ensuring the product is in a location where the consumer expects it—such as selling alcohol in vending machines—and is available when the consumer needs the product.

One of the crucial elements of distribution that must be taken into account when considering how cultural differences might affect distribution is the perception of distribution in another culture. Most typically, this perception is either of distribution as adding cost or adding value. In the United States we generally view distribution as only adding cost to our products. This is clearly borne out by the popularity of outlet malls—whose premise is that we are dealing more or less directly with the manufacturer that results in us getting a better product for a lower price. Research shows that this perception is largely false—outlet malls do not necessarily offer us cheaper products, but if that's what we believe that's what we act on as consumers.

Alternatively some cultures consider the distribution channel to add value to the product—as is the case of rice stores in Japan. These retailers can be found in some of the most expensive commercial retail areas of Tokyo, yet all they sell—apart from soda in the odd soft drink machine—is rice. The cost of operating such an expensive retail outlet is reflected in the price of the rice, but in the Japanese culture the value they place on rice and the store's ability to provide a wide range of brands, along with storing and grading it properly, is viewed as an important part of the overall product value.

Price—which represents the conversion of the product into revenue—can be affected by cultural differences as well. We must ensure that the actual price accurately reflects the way in which the product has been positioned in the market. Positioning the product in a way that is inconsistent with the price charged is an easy mistake to make. We need to avoid mistakes like telling the market our product is "affordable" and then proceed to charge a relatively high price for it—$10 might not be a lot in our home market, but it may be a substantial sum in another market. It could be argued that this perspective of price in more related to economic differences, but it is the cultural values that will define concepts like *value* and *affordable*. A potential problem that is much more directly related to cultural differences is the country-of-origin effect. When consumers in another market make attributes—especially negative attributes—about a product simply based on where the product is produced those determinations are rooted in cultural values. It makes no difference whether or not these perceptions are based in fact—if people believe them they will act upon those beliefs. Korean cars have a pretty decent reliability and quality record, but it has only been fairly recently that American car buyers have had anything other than a relatively negative opinion of these products—and this has been changed through the efforts of the Korean auto manufacturers through heavy promotional campaigns and extended warranties. Much of your success is predicated on the perception of your product—fact-based or not—and your price must not contradict these beliefs unless your firm is willing to actively attempt to change them.

SUMMARY

In summary, what are the keys for success in operating in another market? Remember that culture is not an insurmountable barrier—a little knowledge goes a long way and cultural differences may not be a threat to your firm and its product offering. Cultural perceptions of your firm and its product are not static and can be changed. Japanese automakers were very effective in changing the U.S. market's perception that they only offered low-price, low-quality cars—the prevailing belief in the 1970s—to the belief that their products, regardless of the brand, were the most reliable and of the highest quality. It is also important that you don't allow your cultural values to impede your decision making in another culture. Not only is it vital to avoid the trap of viewing cultural differences as right or wrong, but success in other cultures is largely dependent upon imagination—for example, what are the different possible uses of your product or different reasons to buy the product? Finally, it is always instructive to consider the failures of other firms in the market, or markets, in which you are operating or considering entering. Even if those firms have a very different product, or wouldn't be considered your direct competitor, they may still be valuable lessons that could help you avoid your own costly mistakes.

NOTES

1. M. Herskovits, *Man and His Works* (Stanford, CA: Stanford University Press, 1948).

2. G. Hofstede, "The Cultural Relativity of Organizational Practices and Theories," *Journal of International Business Studies* 14 (1983): 75–89.

3. B. Keillor and T. Hult, "A Five-Country Study of National Identity: Implications for International Marketing Research and Practice," *International Marketing Review* 16, no. 1 (1999): 65–82.

PART II

PLANNING FOR THE INTERNATIONAL MARKETPLACE

.

5

Market Selection: Choosing Your Destination

INTRODUCTION

Arriving at the point where you and your firm begin to consider which markets to operate in and how to operationally enter those new markets represents the first major strategic decision in international business. Up to this point we have considered the impact of various differences in the business environment and how they might impact our business model. We have also considered the important issues related to assessing our firm's potential vulnerability in nondomestic markets. All of these represent vital preliminary issues that must be taken into account prior to making any tangible moves into international markets. The next step, market selection and entry strategy, is a significant departure from our discussion to this point, and these are very closely tied together. Now we are no longer viewing potential markets from an arms-length viewpoint, so to speak. Once the discussion turns to market entry we are now beginning to make decisions such as which market to enter, what entry strategy fits our circumstances the best, and when is the best time to enter our chosen market or markets.

THE MARKET SELECTION PROCESS

These are the three basic questions that must be addressed in making strategic decisions to enter a nondomestic market. The first, which market—or markets—to enter, is vital as it is the decision upon which your international business model rests. Our earlier discussions of the various elements of the market environment—economics, politics, culture, demographics, competition, and technology—all come into play when selecting a market as do other issues. For example, in addition to the characteristics of the market environment we also must take into account our objectives, strategies, and tactics. This means making some determinations regarding our projected outcomes—short term and long term, our priorities, and, if operations in multiple markets are being contemplated, which country at which time and why. At this point we have covered these areas of the business environment. In this chapter and the next we will begin to apply what we have discussed in the context of market selection and market entry strategies.

The second question, addressed in the next chapter, involves the scale or scope of our market operations; that is, by what means will you enter your international market(s). Put another way, operationally how will you present your firm and its products to those new markets? Are you planning to make a major strategic commitment (keeping in mind that there are good reasons for varying the level of commitment to international operations)? Alternatively, are you planning a limited market entry to "test the waters"? Finally, will your firm take the traditional route, beginning with exporting, or use a more committed approach? The traditional route of initiating international operations with exporting has some real advantages—avoiding start-up and in-country manufacturing costs and the ability to gain market experience with a relatively low level of resource commitment—but also some substantial disadvantages (i.e., tariffs and other trade barriers, high transportation costs, and potentially higher production costs).

The third question, which involves using your assessment of the international environment discussed in Chapters 1–4, is when will you enter the market? Like many areas of business the key to success in international business can be found in timing. Here we need to think about questions like what is the climate in the market relative to nondomestic firms. Is the market ready for your product and the way your firm operates? What is the status of your competition and from where—the local market, your home market, or an outside market—does your competition originate? There is also the issue of possible first-mover advantage. Being the first to provide a particular good or service in a market can represent some real advantages—the preemption of your competition, the ease of capturing market share, increased customer loyalty, and even higher switching costs for your consumers. But there are other disadvantages to being first in a market that, while perhaps easy to overlook, can be serious as well. These could potentially include time, money, and other resources that must be expended in order to adequately learn the market(s) along with the time and money associated with educating your new customers—as well as the costs that might be incurred through mistakes as your firm moves along the learning curve.

THE PHYSICAL ENVIRONMENT AND MARKET SELECTION

The actual physical environment of a market is the one key aspect of the international business environment that we have not yet addressed. A discussion of the physical environment involves its external location relative to your current markets of operation and the physical characteristics of the market and their impact on your firm's operations. At the highest level, the physical environment can affect your firm's response time to changes in the market, the risks associated with greater physical distance between your home and host market(s), and the actual physical setting in which business is conducted.

The process of selecting a market is very similar to the process consumers work through in creating an evoked set of products. When consumers create an evoked set of products they recognize that not every product on the market will meet their wants and needs. So in order to get a more reasonable grasp on the different alternatives, the consumer will use a variety of criteria to eliminate products from consideration—creating an evoked set. In a similar vein, firms contemplating operations outside their home market will recognize that not every country in the world is equally viable. Thus the need to create this evoked set of potential markets. Before we can engage the actual market selection process with the goal of creating an evoked set of potential markets, it is first helpful to consider some of the key elements of the physical environment that will influence our market selection as well as how the physical environment can influence the various functional areas of international business.

The actual physical location of a market under consideration is the best place to begin. This external location, relative to your firm's current market, or markets, of operation has a real impact on the attractiveness of that market and these issues can be taken into account quickly, and without any significant resource expenditure. Proximity to your current operational locations is vital given the potential problems, mentioned above, related to response time and distance risk. In addition, assuming the markets that are potential operational targets don't have "perfect proximity" (i.e., are located directly adjacent to your home market) we must take into account not only the actual proximity but also the other countries that stand between our home market and those potential host markets.

Depending upon the nature of your product and the entry strategy selected, these neighboring markets can represent threats in the form of trade barriers to the movement of goods or even direct risk to your product itself. In developing an evoked set of potential markets and selecting the market(s) deemed most attractive before the analysis of those markets' internal physical characteristics can be performed we must recognize that trade relationships between your home market and these neighboring markets can affect the attractiveness of adjacent markets as can the political relationships between your home market, your potential host market, and these countries that are located, literally, in the path of your proposed international operations.

Internally, we must think about how we intend to engage in international operations. If this involves the movement of goods within each market of operation then the topography of countries must enter the equation as should climate and the environment itself. Related to this would be the existing infrastructure's ability to deal with the physical environment in areas such as movement of product, movement of human resources and information, mobility of consumers, production capabilities, and product usage capabilities as well as natural resource requirements and both their availability and accessibility. We must also account for the urban geography of the market—population distribution and density—and the human geography—demographics, education, literacy, birth rates, death rates, and so forth—as the people who live in a country represent a facet of the physical environment as well. The physical environment of a market can explain much in terms of a given market's economic development and attractiveness to outside firms.

HOW CAN THE PHYSICAL ENVIRONMENT IMPACT INTERNATIONAL BUSINESS?

Before we take the next step and begin the discussion of the market selection process, taking just a moment to reinforce the importance of the process might be worthwhile. Consider for a minute the four primary functional areas of business: accounting, finance, management, and marketing. Each can be directly, and significantly, affected by the physical environment of the market in which the firm operates. One of the major responsibilities of the accounting function with a firm is dealing with taxes. Just one small area of the physical environment can have a profound effect on the company's tax liability—an aging population. Most developed markets in the world face the problem of an aging population. What we often forget in the United States is that these markets also have more comprehensive social networks than in this country—health care being a mainstay. As a country's population ages, the need for health care—and health care funding—increases oftentimes with a resulting increase in taxes (tax increases on nondomestic companies very often being placed at the front of the line). Thus, a change on human geography places a strain on the firm's accounting systems. Financial management can be similarly affected. A lack of stability in the physical environment, for example, the propensity of a market to suffer earthquakes à la Japan can reduce the value of assets and investments or increase the cost of doing business. Changing demographics can affect human resource management through changes in the available workforce or changes in the benefits demanded by employees.

Even what appears, at least on the surface, to be an insignificant physical characteristic of a given market can seriously impact marketing activities. For example, two markets with essentially the same overall business environment characteristics—such as the auto market in the United States and the United Kingdom—can be very different simply due to the physical nature of each country. In the United States the average annual mileage put on a car is about 15,000 miles. Because it is geographically so small, the average annual mileage put on a car in the United Kingdom is about one-third of that figure. If mileage is an indicator of product age, cars in the United States age much faster meaning a replacement will be more likely to be purchased—all else being equal—in the United States than the United Kingdom. Faced with this, car manufacturers selling in the United Kingdom can either accept the fact that their products will turn over much slower than in the United States or find a means other than odometer mileage to motivate their customers to buy a replacement.

THE MARKET SELECTION PROCESS: PRELIMINARY ISSUES

Prior to engaging in the market selection process we must first take into account the preliminary issues tied to choosing your market(s). These preliminary issues are straightforward: what is your firm looking for in your international markets? This can be reduced down to three areas of attention—marketing, production, and strategy.

The preliminary issues related to marketing have to do with what your firm may be looking for in a market as it relates to revenue generation. Is your firm looking for a market, or markets, where concerns over time, distance, and setting are minimized (thereby reducing some of the product delivery risks associated with the physical environment)? Or is the most important issue the characteristics of your target market (i.e., human and urban geography)? Another key issue that needs to be considered is any product synergies that might be achieved in the right market—that is, how important to your firm is it to identify markets that require minimal product adaptation? The goal here is to determine how important is a market's potential to directly increase revenue to your firm's international objectives.

The production-related issues are more focused on the attractiveness of a given market in terms of achieving operational goals. Here we are not directly concerned with the market's ability to generate revenue and sales but rather with the characteristics it possesses that could potentially improve operational effectiveness and efficiency. As was the case with the marketing issues, reducing time and distance risk is also a production issue. However, from the perspective of production we are not concerned with our ability to deliver a product; rather the production side is most interested in reducing time and distance as a means of reducing the production costs associated with extended supply and manufacturing lines. Similarly, there is also the area of production costs related to labor—actual labor costs, labor availability, labor expertise, and so forth, as well as the extent to which the product must be "localized." This would address the problem of product content and inputs—not those such as reducing country-of-origin effect that are marketing issues. Production-related market characteristics do not focus directly on revenue generation à la marketing issues but on the degree to which the firm's international operations can achieve maximum operational efficiencies.

The third issue deals with strategy. Before we can create an evoked set of markets and effectively assess these markets your firm will need to have a clear vision of what is expected from international operations. This goes back to our opening discussion in Chapter 1, particularly as it relates to your international objectives. In other words, why—exactly—is your firm engaging in international operations? Is the goal primarily to increase revenue and sales or reduce production costs? Or are you simply trying to off-load excess inventory? Where do your firm's international operations fit into its total operations? Are you already operating in other nondomestic markets? What lessons have you learned that can be applied to this new market?

All three of these categories of preliminary issues related to market selection have a single common theme. Before we can truly assess a market we need to know what your firm intends to get out of that market. Knowing what we realistically expect should increase the quality of your evoked set of potential markets and your final selection of markets to enter.

THE MARKET SELECTION PROCESS: INPUT VARIABLES

The first input variables to consider—market size and sales potential—directly relate to the evaluation of a potential market primarily as a revenue-generating destination. However, there are also elements to take into account here that could impact the market's attractiveness as an operational location as well. Here we are going to actually apply much of your assessment of the economic environment in a specific context. Taking the information and analysis of the market's economy we now ask how the income indicators—disposable income and income expenditures in the area of product type—relate to your firm's product offering. Does this potential market have not only the quantity, but also the quality, of demand necessary to make the market viable? In addition, what are the income and population trends that would indicate the sustainability of that demand? Last, and this would affect both revenue and operational goals, what is the level of economic development and industrialization? The former would provide insight into the stability of demand over time and the latter insight into the type of operational environment the market might provide.

Next we take a careful look at external and internal operational characteristics of the market. This means both the market itself and how well your firm "matches" the market in question. The assessment of external operational capabilities is about seeking out similarities in geography, culture/language, and the market. Basically the task is this: determine the extent to which the market being assessed is operationally similar to your home market. Geographic similarities are concerned with not just the similarity of the location (i.e., it can reasonably be concluded that a market that is in close proximity to your home market has a similar physical environment when it comes to topography and climate) but also the urban and human geography, the infrastructure, and the availability and accessibility of natural resources. Culture and language similarities focus on the firm's ability to communicate in the market—not just language differences but the mechanics of communication such as language difficulties encountered in Asian markets with the differing means of written communication. For example, the Japanese market uses three character-based alphabets: the Kanji (traditional Chinese characters), the Hiragana (a 46-character phonetic alphabet for spelling native Japanese words), and the Katakana (a 46-character phonetic alphabet for spelling non-Japanese words). All three of these alphabets can be used in a single sentence making written communication a challenge that extends beyond just understanding the words themselves. Market similarities, such as the level of economic development, are also important not just because of their influence on market size and sales potential (discussed above) but because markets of similar economic development are typically very similar operational environments meaning firms do not have to substantially change the way in which they operate in order to enter these markets.

Internal operational compatibility relates to matching the company's operational resource base with what is required for success in that market. This means taking into consideration the extent to which the market's demands are consistent with the firm's capabilities. For example, a small Midwestern software firm passed on a contract in Puerto Rico that would have doubled the company's annual revenue. The problem? The client in Puerto Rico required the software have a Spanish-language interface. Because the firm had no Spanish-speaking programmers, was not confident in its ability to oversee translation issues, and did not find an investment in those areas to be in the firm's long-term best interest, it left a large pile of cash on the table— opting instead to focus on marketing its software in Great Britain where language capabilities were not required.

The types of resources the firm has access to, especially financial and human expertise/knowledge, is also an important determinant in selecting the proper market to enter. As highlighted in the software example above, it is not always the availability of finances that can restrict the number of viable markets. The issue at hand is not the compatibility of the market with the firm's existing resources; it is about maximizing your firm's resources by assessing what might be leveraged for the greatest effect. Again, using the software firm as an example, being a small firm it did not have large amounts of capital to invest in international operations. However, the firm did possess a very high level of programming skills especially in the area of developing easy-to-operate user interfaces. This meant that once the language barrier had been overcome—or in this company's case removed from the equation—the firm could leverage its ability to make its product easy to use and gain competitive advantage in its new European market.

The final input variable involves placing much of our previous discussions related to assessment of the various components of the international business environment into a context that is directly applicable to helping us address a specific issue. Now we are talking about taking what we have learned from certain aspects of the international business environment—specifically our analysis of the extent to which your firm faces competitive, economic/monetary, and political risk. Remember, we are using this information to help determine which markets under consideration might enter into your evoked set of markets that might be selected for international operations.

In the area of the competitive environment we need to know how much competition your firm can anticipate (i.e., the number of potential competitors and the amount of market share they may already hold in the market) but we also need to ascertain how willing the competition is to fight for that market (i.e., their market priorities). This is a crucial area to consider as your primary competitor(s) may not be local firms. However, that does not mean these competitors are willing to engage resources to retain their hold in that market. Often firms will enter another market simply because it is relatively easy to operate in (i.e., competition-free). These companies will generate as much revenue as possible as quickly as possible and when more competitors enter they simply move on to another market. Thus, the presence of competitors does not always mean they place the same priority on a given market as your firm, suggesting the market may be more attractive than it appears at first glance.

For the purposes of market entry decisions, the term *monetary* refers to the aspects of the economic environment that would impact the firm's revenue generation both short and long term. Short-term monetary considerations would center on the characteristics of the market that would affect the liquidity of the revenue earned in the market. Not only the form of the revenue—is it in the form of liquid assets (i.e., money) or some type of countertrade—but also the portability of that revenue (e.g., the existence of revenue repatriation restrictions that prevent your firm from taking its earnings out of the market). Long-term monetary issues are directed at the sustainability of your revenue stream—considerations directed at the stability of not only customer demand but also the stability of the market in general.

The third area under this heading of risk assessment would be political risk. As recent events in the Middle East have shown, risk related to the system of government, leadership, external relations with other countries, and disaffected groups in the country can all contribute to the creation of a market that is fundamentally unstable. As we looked at in length in Chapter 3, the political environment is complex and the threats with which it is associated can represent considerable risk to a firm and suggest that, if these risks are present, the market in question may not be the best choice for your firm's international operation.

THE MARKET SELECTION PROCESS: CHOICE

Once the evoked set of markets determined to be reasonable options for your firm's international operations has been constructed, the question turns to which of the markets will be selected. Here is where the concept of an evoked set of markets departs from the concept of an individual consumer's evoked set of products. In the latter it is a given that the consumer will select only one product. In the case of the evoked set of markets your firm is faced with a more complex situation—do you select only one market, more than one from the evoked set, or all of the markets in that evoked set?

This is a question of market diversification versus market concentration. On one end of the spectrum is market diversification. When a firm chooses to adopt a market diversification approach to its market selection strategy it is opting to operate in more than one, perhaps all, markets in its evoked set. It could be argued that a market diversification approach would require substantial resources given that the firm has chosen to operate in multiple international markets. This market diversification approach does necessitate more resources be devoted to international operations as the number of markets selected for operations increases. This, in turn, often means that growth in any one of those markets may be relatively slow.

However, like a diversification strategy in investments, a market diversification strategy can be one that has less risk. If any one, or some combination of, markets becomes less attractive—for whatever reasons—the firm's entire international operations are not immediately compromised. This can be an attractive market selection strategy if your firm's products are found to be associated with risk—physical or social hazards—or your firm's operations are considered to have a negative impact on local firms—a situation where relatively slow and relatively small-scale operations draw less unfavorable attention to your firm.

A market concentration selection strategy is just the opposite of a market diversification approach. When a firm chooses a market concentration strategy it has decided to focus on one, or a very limited number, of markets with the intent of obtaining fast growth in the market(s) entered. This market selection strategy is most suited to firms who have identified certain unique characteristics of a market that match well with their product offering and also have the potential for significant market opportunities. For example, Foster's Lager determined several years ago that one of the unique positive characteristics of its beer was the country of origin: Australia. The company decided to concentrate on a very limited number of markets around the globe that represented large revenue opportunities but also required a tailored business model; that is, the markets selected (of which the United States was one) had a positive view of all things Australian resulting in the firm equating its product with Australia ("Foster's—Australian for Beer"). Concentrating on a limited number of markets can be very risky—a lot of resources could be lost if your firm's analysis of this small number of markets is incorrect—but it also has the potential for significant profits. As we saw in a previous chapter, for Foster's Lager it meant being able to break its home market positioning of a low-end beer and reinvent itself as a relatively high-priced premium product in the United States.

In making this choice of diversification or concentration, or some middle ground, your firm should consider several factors. First there are factors related to the long-term viability of the market itself—particularly growth rate, sources of growth, and sales stability. The best markets are those that not only represent opportunity now, but also will be able to maintain this attractiveness over time. Obviously it is impossible to foresee all possible events and circumstances that might negatively impact a market but, as we have seen in looking at the various aspects of the international business environment, it is possible to identify possible problem areas. Second are the factors related to the competition and competitive advantage. The important issues of identifying the competition, the source advantages these competitors might enjoy, and the extent to which they are willing to fight your firm for market share are crucial. So is having a firm grip on what gives your firm unique competitive advantage and the possible product and operational synergies that might be obtained in certain markets. Finally, there is the issue of how well your company and product "fit" in the market. Does a significant country-of-origin effect exist? Does your product fill, or have the ability to fill, a specific need of that market? Also, what is the climate in general toward nondomestic firms in that market? All of these factors form the basis for the market choice criteria you should utilize.

In making the market selection decision it is also advisable to take into account the two most common errors. On one hand, firms can sometime overlook market opportunities. This involves excluding a market, or markets, from the evoked set of markets oftentimes due to subjectivity such as allowing the self-reference criterion to influence decision making or stereotyping the market based on other characteristics such as economic indicators (e.g., income). On the other hand, it is also possible to include too many markets in the evoked set. This is not the result of subjectivity but rather a lack of focus. Firms that consider too many markets typically have unfocused goals when it comes to their international operations, what they are trying to accomplish, and the resources they can reasonably commit—now and in the future.

SUMMARY

In the discussion of international business to this point it could be easy to overlook the fact that we have not yet considered the markets in which we will operate. This chapter deals with this issue. Beginning with an overview of the market selection process, the chapter covers how the physical environment impacts the market selection process as well as how it can affect the functional areas of business. The preliminary issues related to the actual selection of a market along with the important variables that influence the process were also discussed. The chapter concludes with the actual choice, or choices, of the appropriate market(s) given your firm's international objectives. The purpose of the chapter is to provide a guideline for selecting an international market for operations and a basis for moving into the next important topic area: market entry strategy.

6

Market Entry: Making Strategic Decisions

INTRODUCTION

There are three basic types of entry strategies available to a firm. These are exporting, partnerships—either vertical or horizontal—and foreign direct investment (FDI). All three of these are legitimate choices for firms with any level of international experience. Too often there is an assumption that firms who engage in exporting are either inexperienced or not fully committed to international operations—something that is simply not true. Exporting can be a good long-term strategy depending upon the firm's international objectives and the resources the firm is willing and able to commit to international operations. Similarly, foreign direct investment has been employed by firms with little experience in international operations, or little willingness to develop an international strategy, but with sufficient financial resources to "buy" its way into a market.

What are these determinants of market entry strategy? They can be classified as either firm-related or market-related. Like many of the issues related to international business and international business strategy, we need to look both at your firm as well as the market in which you intend to operate in order to find the right fit. In this case the fit we are looking for is a match of the firm's characteristics and capabilities with the market through the choice of the best market entry strategy. The firm-related characteristics come, not in the form of the firm's current business model, but rather in the form of strategy variables that the firm may or may not be able to leverage in the global marketplace. The market-related characteristics, on the other hand, represent environment variables unique to a specific market that may make one approach to market entry more attractive than the alternatives.

FIRM-RELATED DETERMINANTS

The firm-related, or strategy variables, that are the market entry strategy determinants unique to your firm relate to the competitive environment in a given market, the means by which your firm can leverage certain synergies, and where your international operations fit into your firm's overall business model. As we have already discussed, the threat raised by competition is not just whether or not competitors are actively present in a market but also the extent to which these competitors are willing to commit resources to fight you in that market. This particular discussion, as it relates to the competitive environment, is referred to as "concentration." In international business we know it as "global concentration." This concept recognizes that your competition may place more emphasis on some markets than others. For example, in the worldwide tire industry Goodyear Tire and Rubber is truly a global manufacturer—accounting for 40 percent of all tires made in the world. But the firm is much more protective of its U.S. market (in particular, its OEM sales to U.S. automakers) than it is in Europe. That is not to say Goodyear doesn't actively compete in the European market; rather all else being equal the firm chooses to engage resources to maintain market share in the United States. instead of Europe when faced with the choice. Similar attitudes are adopted by large European tire companies such as Michelin.

When faced with a potential market that will be actively defended by your competition, rather than immediately adopting an "all in" market entry strategy it might be advisable to quietly learn the market without identifying your firm as an immediate threat. This is how Japanese tire manufacturers first entered the U.S. market—by exporting tires that were not direct threats to what were at the time the dominant firms in the market: Goodyear and Firestone. Focusing initially on niche or specialty products, such as motorcycle tires—a product market in which Goodyear and Firestone were not interested—meant the Japanese firms could learn the U.S. market (consumers, promotion, distribution, etc.) without having to immediately fight their way in against these two dominant and established rivals. Over time, the Japanese firms were able to position themselves in the market and—having built a solid understanding of the market along with recognized brand equity—they were able to make more aggressive moves. In particular, Bridgestone simply used its market knowledge and superior resource base to acquire Firestone thus moving from exporting into substantial direct investment in the market.

There is also the issue of global synergy to consider. Global synergy refers to the ability of your core product to be leveraged in ways otherwise not viable in your home market. The key to achieving global synergy is to have a clear understanding of your core product competency—that is, what your firm does especially well that is reflected in your product and that can also be adapted in a variety of ways. For example, Honda's core product competency is the design and manufacture of small internal combustion engines. A brief review of the company history shows that starting with motorcycles as its large market product, moving into automobiles—the first of which were powered by motorcycle engines—and then the company's expansion into a myriad of other products, the recurring theme has been products built around the firm's engine design and manufacture ability. As the firm expanded its product line it realized that many of these engine-based products are not well suited for the home market of Japan. There is simply not much demand for products such as power lawnmowers, outboard motors, and so forth in Japan. However, there are markets around the world, such as the United States, where these products do have sizable and sustainable demands. The decision was made by Honda to invest directly in the United States in order to be close to the market demand for these products that were based on the firm's core competency but had little demand in the home market.

Before we move on to the market-related variables that are determinants of your firm's market entry strategy, there is one more firm-related variable to cover—your firm's international strategic goal(s). Your market entry strategy must be consistent with the overall goals that have been established for your international operations. If the long-term goal is to establish a base for revenue-generation then exporting might be a good first step, but more involved market entry strategies such as host firm partnerships or even foreign direct investment may be called for as your firm's market presence develops. Alternatively, if the objective is simply to use international markets as a place to off-load excess inventory or somehow defray other operational costs then a lower level of commitment (i.e., exporting) would be the logical choice. Market entry strategy, like so many other aspects of international business, has several options—all of which can be both good or bad choices depending upon the match between your firm and the choices available.

MARKET-RELATED DETERMINANTS

The market-related, or environmental, variables that help determine the appropriate market entry strategy for your firm are not unique or specific to your firm—to a large extent these are issues that other firms from your home market will see much the same as your firm regardless of their industry. Taking into account these market-related variables involves revisiting the information and analysis already completed in the assessment of the various pieces of the business environment. Country risk—particularly political and economic—must be brought into the equation. Clearly, the higher the level of country risk the less it would make sense to place difficult-to-move assets in that country. Related to country risk is the potential problem of demand uncertainty—current and future. Like country risk, as demand uncertainty increases so does the likelihood that your firm's best market entry strategy options might be those that enable higher levels of asset protection and control à la exporting.

There is also a need, when considering the various market entry strategy options, to take time to assess your individuals firm's familiarity with the proposed market location. Does your firm have experience in similar markets that can be effectively leveraged for success in the market under consideration? What level of expertise does your firm have that can be brought to bear to increase the likelihood of success? Finally, what mistakes other firms—home, host, and outside—have made can your firm learn from? To some extent this issue of familiarity is one of resource availability but unlike many international business challenges the resources that are most valuable in this case are not necessarily financial resources—they are very likely to be the knowledge and expertise-based resources that your firm currently possesses.

MARKET ENTRY STRATEGY OPTIONS

At the opening of the previous section we established that there are three basic market entry strategy options: exporting, partnerships, and foreign direct investment. While some argue that these represent a progression of the degree to which a firm is internationalized—moving from exporting to partnerships and finally to foreign direct investment—we are going to avoid this characterization. The reason is simple: to suggest that a firm at the exporting level is less "internationalized" than one engaged in foreign direct investment is misleading. For many very experienced, internationally committed firms exporting is the very best market entry strategy choice. Much of what makes the best market entry strategy choice is closely tied to your firm's international marketing strategy—particularly as it relates to product positioning—but we will deal with that discussion later. For now our focus is on understanding the market entry strategy choices that are available and what your firm must take into account in order for any of these options to be effective.

EXPORTING AS AN ENTRY STRATEGY

Exporting is generally considered to be the first step when a firm decides to place its product into an international market. This is because of the three market entry options available, exporting can be initiated much faster than either partnerships or direct investment and it also requires fewer resources. At the most basic level exporting can be defined as "build it here, sell it there." Shortly we shall see that exporting is much more complicated than that, but this simple definition does capture the essence of exporting; that is, beyond its speed and costs advantages exporting allows a firm to maintain as much control over its operations and products as keeping these in its home market. That is one of the significant advantages of exporting—control. Another key advantage to exporting is its ability to maintain your firm and its products' positive country-of-origin associations. Finally, unlike the other market entry strategies, exporting can be done internally by your firm, an activity known as *direct* exporting, or your firm can choose to engage an export management company to conduct your export program—referred to as "indirect" exporting.

Many established international firms have never moved beyond exporting as an entry strategy for the very good reason that by having their product identified as "imported" they are able to charge a premium price for that product. Exporting is a viable long-term market entry strategy, but for it to be effective you and your firm must carefully consider the tasks that must be performed in the exporting process. Here is where exporting can become very complex. If your firm decides to opt for maximum control in its market entry activities through a direct exporting entry strategy then it must be willing and capable of performing all these necessary export tasks—often a daunting proposition for a firm, particularly one with little or no international experience.

The need to ensure that the exporting tasks are performed and performed properly over time is the biggest reason firms will cede control, and a substantial portion of the profits in a market, to an export management company—thereby engaging in indirect exporting. What, then, are these tasks? They go far beyond just the physical movement of product. This is where characterizing exporting as "built it here, sell it there" becomes an oversimplification. Both aspects of this simple definition are far more involved—which we will see as we consider the necessary tasks of exporting.

Exporting—Logistical Tasks

These tasks can be placed into one of three categories—logistical, transactional, and support. Logistical activities are the tasks most commonly associated with exporting. As the label indicates, logistical tasks involve the movement of product. The first issue that must be addressed in order to "sell it there" is the shipment of the product from the home country of manufacture to the targeted host country. Product shipment means much more than packing and moving. The task that must be effectively completed is moving the product across what are often large geographic distances using multiple transportation methods and ensuring that the product has not been damaged or lost—that is, the product is marketable when it reaches the market. This involves ensuring not only that the product is properly packaged for shipment, but also having procedures in place to account for the product's safe and timely movement to the host market. It also means that there are safety nets in place—often in the form of insurance—to protect the firm against any product damage or loss. Put quite simply, if the product does not reach the host market in sufficient quantities and in a condition that is "sellable" your product has failed in the market before it even reached the distributors and final customers.

Upon delivery to the market, the second major logistical task that must be discharged is local distribution. It is one thing to ensure the product reaches the host market—it is something else entirely to disseminate your product throughout that market. Think of the situation in these terms: in having your product reach the host market in a marketable form your firm has accomplished little more than what it would have achieved had the product been manufactured at home and shipped from the factory to the next step in the distribution channel. The considerable task of getting the product to the customer still remains.

Frequently, accomplishing the task of local distribution is the most difficult for the firm who chooses to employ direct exporting. This is where the export management firm can become invaluable. It is often well worth the foregone revenue—sometimes as much as one-third of sales—to have access to a well-established distribution channel. The functions and role of this distribution channel, one of the parts of the overall value chain, will be covered in detail in the next chapter but for our purposes here consider this: the task of local distribution is all about creating and maintaining an effective link with your customer in what is very often an unfamiliar market environment. Just as the product shipment task must be performed thoroughly and efficiently in order to ensure your firm actually has a product to market, the local distribution function must be completely at the same high level in order to establish and manage your firm's connection with the customer base in this new market—and ensure that connection will last over time.

Exporting—Transactional Tasks

The next category of export tasks—transactional—cannot be performed without the establishment of a structure for the logistical tasks. In other words, if your firm has not ensured that these logistical tasks can be effectively completed then addressing the transactional tasks is a waste of time. Put another way, without the logistics in place no transactions will occur. These transactional tasks are not concerned with initiating the transactions; this is done through the connection with customers established through the local distribution task and supported by the next set of tasks—support. The transactional tasks, like the logistical, seem straightforward. However, also like the logistical tasks, they are more complicated than they might first appear and they are crucial. Failure of these transactional tasks means failure in the market.

The transactional tasks are payment collection and after-the-sale support. Collecting sales receipts may sound easy, but consider this: your firm is trying to ensure it receives all the monies due from members of a distribution channel with which it is likely unfamiliar, in a market where its knowledge base is not well developed, in a currency that—at some point—will have to be converted into your home currency and then moved somehow back to your home market. Payment collection, especially if your firm decides on direct exporting, is much more than cashing a check. Again, if any of these crucial payment collection issues are beyond the scope of your firm—and you had better be very confident in your firm's ability to accomplish these activities—indirect exporting becomes the most credible choice.

In order to maintain a viable presence over time in the host market, after-the-sale service must also enter the equation. Too often firms will approach this by concluding that after-the-sale service is not an issue. Perhaps in your home market your product does not require any real service support. Maybe your firm has determined that an absence of real competition means that it does not need to provide service support. These are just two examples of the reasoning firms will apply for not providing service support—the real reason being that service support can be a real problem to coordinate and provide without incurring substantial costs. However, your firm cannot avoid what service support represents—the means of maintaining good relationships in the market. The competitive intensity of the global marketplace requires all firms to look beyond moving from transaction to transaction and developing a basis for attracting and retaining customers through a relationship-based customer model. Further, the differences across markets may mean that customers in the host market—whether they are individuals or businesses—demand higher levels of service support than your home market. Keeping in mind that as an outside firm you will likely be held at a higher standard, at least until your products are established in the market, that will in turn require your firm to be much more relational in its dealing with customers and service support is the vehicle to create that type of relationship.

Exporting—Support Tasks

The last set of tasks—support—is easy to overlook. These can be administrative tasks such as dealing with shipping invoices, insuring product shipments, and other paperwork that moves product to the final customer. There is also the issue of legal tasks—such as contracts—that are associated with not only the movement of goods but also ensuring the product will clear customs and pass all the necessary regulations and restrictions. Lastly, there is the issue of promotional support and the other activities that must be provided within the distribution channel in order to ensure your product is not only made effectively accessible to your customers but also presented in such a way as to be competitive with alternative products. Taken in total, the tasks that must be performed for an exporting program to be successful can be intimidating—all the more reason to carefully consider each in detail before selecting direct exporting as your firm's market entry strategy of choice.

Beyond these necessary export tasks there are some other factors to consider when making the final decision of whether to engage in direct exporting or to employ an indirect exporting approach. Firm resources are an obvious factor to consider—the tasks required of an effective exporting program represent substantial resource commitment. On the other hand, indirect exporting not only places these responsibilities on the export management company, but payments to these companies are commonly tied to product sales, meaning your firm's cash outlay is not wholly upfront but a portion of successful product sales. There is also the nature of the product to consider. To what extent does your product require special handling, customization, or after-sale service? As these special requirements go up so does the desired level of control your firm may wish to maintain in the host market. The existence of international experience and expertise within your firm can be an important determinant of the type of exporting program best suited to your firm. Those with previous international market experience find that they are much better suited to direct exporting as market entry strategy knowledge is an area of international operations that can "translate" from what would otherwise be very divergent markets. Finally, the business conditions in your selected market may suggest one exporting form over the other. For example, in markets where there may be negative attitudes toward nondomestic firms it might be advisable to engage in indirect exporting and have your firm represented by a local distributor. Alternatively, a high level of brand recognition in the host market may mean that direct exporting is the best way for your firm to maintain control of its product image.

PARTNERSHIPS AS AN ENTRY STRATEGY

While exporting has some distinct advantages as a market entry strategy, it is not always the best choice for all firms. Given the task that must be performed either directly by the firm or indirectly managed by the firm, exporting, as we have seen, is not as easy as it might appear on the surface. There are other drawbacks to exporting as well—one of the biggest being that exporting does not establish the type of connection with the international market that can be used to gain the competitive advantage associated with operating in the market. Often the notion of operating within a market is thought of in terms of foreign direct investment. While that is certainly an option there is a middle ground for market entry. Some form of partnership with a local firm or individual can allow your firm to extend itself into that market and garner the advantages identified with being operationally placed in that market and, at the same time, avoid some of the risks associated with direct investment along with avoiding the resource expenditures that also go along with direct investment.

The goal of a market entry partnership is to have the advantages of a localized operation. There are a number of advantages that go along with localized operations depending upon how each individual firm decides to construct these host market partnerships. However, there are several advantages that can be obtained no matter how the individual arrangement is created. One is the market knowledge—both current and future—that can be obtained through some form of partnership. Exporting provides experience in a host market, but the usefulness of that experience is oftentimes limited to the more mechanical operational areas in a market such as dealing with customs regulation for the admittance of your product. Certainly this operational knowledge is valuable, but it does not have the strategic value that a local partner can provide. Knowledge of customers, market trends, the competition, and the political environment can all be accessed through a local partner—knowledge that may never be fully gathered using exporting as a market entry strategy. There is also another key advantage—by entering into some type of partnership arrangement it may be possible for your firm to remove or reduce any identification it has in the market as a "foreign" company.

As we consider the different partnership options it is important to be clear that the specifics of an individual partnership between your firm and a host firm can vary widely. In fact, in any given market it could be argued that no two market entry partnership agreements look the same. Having said that, there are some broad types of market entry partnerships as well as some core dimensions that are associated with functional and effective partnerships.

Vertical versus Horizontal Partnerships

Generally, market entry partnerships can be characterized as being either "vertical" or "horizontal." Vertical partnerships are those where one member—frequently the nondomestic firm—has more control in the agreement; that is, the functioning and success of the partnership is dependent upon that firm. The most common of these vertical partnerships are licensing or franchising agreements and contract manufacturing. A licensing agreement is a contractual arrangement whereby one firm permits another to use a portion of its business model or product. For example, one very common type of franchise agreement over the years has been the licensing of a brand name. The primary advantage to the firm owning the brand is the ability to place that brand very quickly into a new market. The licensing firm in the host market then receives what is already a successful brand. Licensing is a good partnership option if your firm possesses something—either tangible or intangible—which gives it competitive advantage and which can be relatively easily transferred.

Franchising takes the licensing agreement further by licensing a complete business model. Franchising has been shown to be a proven and successful market entry strategy particularly for firms with a business model that is well suited for a "think global, act local" approach to international operations. Oftentimes the companies with a substantial service component to their product find franchising an ideal market entry strategy as it allows the local partner/franchisee to make the necessary changes to the service, or interactive, component of the product. Like franchising, contract manufacturing also works best with certain types of firms—those whose primary business activity is centered on product manufacture. If your business is primarily built around producing a tangible good, contract manufacturing is a market entry strategy that deserves consideration. In addition to the variety of logistical and cost-saving advantages associated with manufacturing your product as close to the customers as possible, contract manufacturing is frequently used to overcome trade barriers and other obstacles that might inhibit the movement of your product from your home market to the host market.

The vertical partnerships—which can be used by firms of all types with a wide range of products—have a single common element. In these vertical partnerships one firm—the firm providing the product—dominates the relationship. In the strategic alliances and joint ventures typically known as horizontal partnerships there is a more equal interaction. The point of departure in the horizontal partnerships in the emphasis on shared ownership and control. A horizontal partnership is distinct in that it is an explicit, long-term partnership where the mutual responsibilities are clearly defined in a formal, legal agreement. Having what amounts to an equal partnership with a local firm enables your firm to potentially tap into the special skills and knowledge it possesses along with gaining sustainable access to customers as well as a distribution network. At the same time, your local partner now has access to your firm's products in addition to the capital advantages both firms enjoy as a result of pooling resources. The key to making these horizontal partnerships work over time comes in the nature of the partnerships. Both a technical and emotional partnership must exist. A technical partnership involves creating a relationship where there are mutual contributions. Note: we are not suggesting that these contributions be equal. A good partnership does not focus on keeping score in terms of dollars invested by each party; rather it is structured so that each side makes significant ongoing contributions that further the partnership's objectives. The emotional partnership involves, not tangible resources, but the desire and commitment on both sides to ensuring the agreement is functional and efficient—that is, a commitment to making it work over time.

Goal Compatibility in Partnerships

Regardless of whether the firm decides upon a vertical or horizontal partnership arrangement, this approach to market entry will only achieve maximum success if certain core dimensions are built in at the outset. One of the most important, yet easily misinterpreted, of these core dimensions is the need to ensure goal compatibility between the two partners. This seems an obvious statement—both partners would not likely enter into the partnership without a mutual goal of success. True. However, the means by which this success is measured can become problematic.

Let's assume the goal of both the home and host country firm in a partnership is to generate revenue within the host market. The question then arises, how will progress toward this goal be evaluated? Here is where it can get complicated. U.S. firms often measure their success in revenue generation through actual sales in a market over a finite time period—quarterly, annual, and so forth. This means the road to success, using sales as a measurement, will be linked to increasing the revenue on each unit sold—a goal that can be reached either through increased cost efficiencies but is often reached in international markets by putting a premium (i.e., relatively high) price on the firm's product. An equally valid means of measuring market success, and the ability of the firm to generate revenue in that market, would be increases in market share. Often this is how firms in Asia determine their long-term market viability. Increasing market share means increasing not number of product units sold but the number of customers captured. The classic means of increasing market share is through a market penetration price (i.e., relatively low). Thus the result is goal incompatibility—one firm attempts to increase profits using a short-term approach while the other uses a long-term approach. Both seek to increase revenue, but the means of accomplishing this goal do not match.

Strategic Advantage in Partnerships

Assuming that the end goal, and the means by which progress toward that goal will be measured, is compatible between the two partner firms, the core dimension of strategic advantage must also be part of the partnership. What we are saying here is that each partner must gain an advantage, through the partnership, that was unattainable without the partnership. An example would be the strategic alliance formed in 2000 between Goodyear Tire and Rubber and Sumitomo Corporation (a Japanese tire firm). Goodyear agreed to approximately $950 million for a share in Sumitomo—a share that was valued at only about $350 million. The strategic advantage to paying so much? For Sumitomo, the answer is obvious—a large infusion of capital. But what about Goodyear? At the time, the company—Goodyear—was experiencing significant cash flow problems.

The notion of borrowing a substantial sum (that is what the firm did) to seemingly overpay for a stake in a Japanese firm on the surface appears to be strategically inadvisable. However, it was strategic advantage that drove the decision. Sumitomo possessed several assets that helped fill strategic gaps for Goodyear. The company was well established in the Japanese market—more than 400 years old—and offered Goodyear an effective means of entering Japan à la Bridgestone's acquisition of Firestone in the 1990s. Sumitomo also had a well-developed line of relatively low-cost aftermarket high-performance tires—a segment Goodyear had targeted as a growth segment but for which the firm's product line at the time was not well developed. Another key asset Goodyear accessed was the Dunlop brand. For a long time Dunlop had been a premier brand particularly in Europe but the brand had not been maintained over the years resulting in loss of market share, but not—interestingly enough—in loss of brand equity. Dunlop represented a valued brand name, a line of performance tires that—if properly marketed—could regain market prominence, and Dunlop tires had been extended into other segments (e.g., motorcycles) that are high margin. Thus, a partnership that might be viewed as one-sided is really one of mutual strategic advantage.

Partnerships: Interdependence, Commitment, and Coordination

Related to strategic advantage are the last three core dimensions for a strategic alliance: interdependence, commitment, and coordination. The concept of interdependence helps to solidify the desired long-term nature of the horizontal partnership. Each firm is dependent upon the other in order to both establish and maintain this long-term agreement. For example, in the classic U.S. firm–host market firm arrangement the host market firm obtains resources such as financial resources and the U.S. firm gains access to distribution and customers in the host market. In the absence of either of these two unique contributions the partnership would cease to be functional—which would not be in the best interest of either firm.

Commitment means that both partners are willing to divert resources from their individual operations to the partnership. No company has unlimited resources so the willingness on the part of each firm to invest a portion of those limited resources into the partnership demonstrates that each is committed to the success of the venture.

Finally, coordination involves the explicit definition within the partnership agreement as to the responsibilities of both firms and how the various strategic and operational issues will be addressed. The issues can generally be placed into one of three separate categories: planning, operations, and conflict resolution. Planning issues deal with both strategies and tactics of the partnerships and the role each party plays in the planning process. Similarly, operations addresses the responsibilities of each party when those plans are implemented in the market. Conflict resolution recognizes that over time disagreements will arise between the two partners and, therefore, the mechanism by which these conflicts will be adjudicated is clearly defined ahead of time.

FOREIGN DIRECT INVESTMENT AS AN ENTRY STRATEGY

Like exporting, in order to be effective as a market entry strategy, a partnership arrangement requires a great deal of effort on the part of both participating companies if it will be successful over time. That being said, the advantages to these partnership agreements can be significant and unique. Unlike exporting and foreign direct investment, partnerships allow for the sharing of resources that may facilitate large strategic and operational investments. Because there must be an element of strategic advantage built into these partnerships both participants will have access to complementary resources (e.g., capital and market access). The partnership allows each firm to share risks, reducing the potential exposure of resources. Lastly, it may allow the two firms to co-opt their competition as one likely source for a partner would be a competing firm. This leads then to the final market entry strategy option: foreign direct investment also known as FDI.

Build versus Buy

Foreign direct investment is the purchase of physical assets or an ownership share in a host market. Alternatively, where exporting is often described as "build it here, sell it there," FDI can be characterized as "build or buy." In either case, foreign direct investment demands a much higher level of resource commitment on the part of the firm than either exporting or partnerships. Some firms will reach the conclusion that the most effective market entry strategy will be one that places their operations directly in the market in which they hope to maximize success. This local placement allows for improved operational efficiencies, a reduction in the market imperfections associated with crossing market borders, and puts the firm and its products as close as possible to the local consumers. In most cases the firms that opt for FDI are those that see in the host market a significant amount of opportunity and that desire to maintain a high level of control over their operations in that host market.

It is often the case that FDI is thought of in terms of "building." That is, the direct investment is in the form of creating physical facilities in the host market. A good example to consider would be BMW's construction of plant facilities in the United States. Building an auto manufacturing facility is clearly a very large investment on the part of the firm, but consider the advantages. The United States is one of the largest markets for SUV sales, particularly high-end models, in the world. It has shown, at least for these types of SUVs, to be not only a large but also a reasonably sustainable market, and by manufacturing those vehicles in the United States the firm can overcome market imperfections as well as any perceptual problems by producing the BMW X5s here in the United States. This is what leads many companies to decide upon a "build" FDI—very close contact to a very large host market. The risks are evident, but it is determined that the return is worth the risk.

Alternatively, some firms will choose to "buy" rather than build. Acquisition of part, or all, of a local firm can in many cases achieve the same results as building and accomplish those results in a much shorter period of time. As is the case with the build option, acquisition demands considerable resources. However, for the firm that has the ability to choose between the two, purchasing local ownership can provide advantages not associated with building. Most notably is the speed at which your firm could become assimilated into the market as a local firm. Consider the example of Walmart in the United Kingdom. Walmart knows that the perception of its firm around the world is probably less favorable than its perception in the United States—one that isn't terrific to begin with. Therefore, in markets where the company seeks large long-term potential it has employed an acquisition approach to FDI. In the United Kingdom the firm purchased an established, but struggling, discount chain known as Asda. This not only gave the firm relatively instant access to the entire U.K. market compared to building stores, but it also provided the added advantage of being able to use an established local name while the stores were gradually adapted to the Walmart business model.

Given the high level of resource commitment, both in real terms as well as the problem of easily divesting the firm of those assets—constructed or acquired—the question becomes what would cause a firm to take on that much risk? The answer is in both the nature of international business and the objectives of individual firms. There is a much higher level of risk and market commitment attached to FDI, but the high levels of control and market potential can be very enticing.

Advantages of Foreign Direct Investment

Let's consider the characteristics of the global marketplace that would cause a firm to conclude that the risk of FDI was more than offset by its return. One issue, that we will address in more detail in the next chapter when we get to product strategy, is that of the product life cycle. More precisely, in what stage of the product life cycle your product is in the host market or markets. A product in the mature stage of the life cycle requires efforts on the part of the firm to maintain its relevance. This most often comes in the form of improved cost efficiencies in the production and marketing of the product or identifying new uses and customer segments for the product. In either case, being able to put your firm's operational activities close to the distributors and customers in the market—in the form of FDI—enables the firm to achieve these goals. Close contact with the market provides the firm with the necessary information and ability to tailor the product to the market's unique needs.

Closely related to the requirements placed on the product by its stage in the product life cycle are the advantages that can be obtained by "internalizing" operations; that is, taking the market imperfections that are an inherent component of doing business across country and market boundaries out of the business equation. Placing much of the activities directed at the local market actually in that local market reduces, or in many cases removes, these market imperfections. Localizing operations can remove the problems of trade barriers and other imperfections that impede the flow of products and make transactions problematic. In addition, localizing as much operational activity in the host market as possible can greatly reduce the impact on costs and revenue that go along with differences in currency exchange rates—and the need to plan for any potential shifts in the stability and predictability of those rates. In many ways it could be argued that an FDI market entry strategy attempts to take as much of the "international" component out of international business as possible.

There is also the notion of location advantage to consider. The advantages associated with locating in that market can come in several forms. There can be "characteristic" advantages related to the characteristics of that market location such as the availability of inputs (e.g., natural resources) or the unique characteristics of the local consumers. There may also be "acquisition" advantages—not necessarily just limited to an acquisition FDI—such as the availability of unique employee skill sets. Finally, there may be "ownership" advantages—not in owning assets in that market but rather unique market advantages attached with what your firm may already possess such as brand equity. Last, beyond the product life cycle, internalization, and location advantages there is the issue of increasing market power. The larger the direct presence a firm has in a host market the greater its ability to command higher levels of market power through more efficient operations designed to capture market share as well as its increased ability to implement operations targeted at increasing operational efficiencies such as forward and/or backward integration.

Finally, there are other advantages a firm can enjoy through direct investment in a host market beyond the ability to maintain control either through the construction or acquisition of assets, the localization of production costs, the ability to gain more valuable customer knowledge, and the reduction of any negative country-of-origin effect. These come in the form of "following." Under most circumstances following in business is identified with being reactive—a formula for losing in many cases. However, following as it relates to FDI can sometimes make good sense. One way of following another firm into a market—and then investing in that market—might be if the firm you are following is your customer. Goodyear has made substantial manufacturing investments in China, recognizing that the firm's single biggest customer—General Motors—now sells more products in China than any other single market. Anticipating that GM will ramp up its local manufacturing in China, Goodyear chose to be as close as possible to that manufacturing. There is also the potential for obtaining *second mover advantage*. In international business discussions there is often a great deal of value attached to what is known as *first mover advantage*—the advantages associated with beating your competition to a market. However, there is also something to be said for learning from other firms' mistakes—especially taking into account the costs attached to ineffective direct investment. Given the large amount of resources required for most foreign direct investment activities, it may be advisable to let another company blaze the trail into the market.

SUMMARY

Market entry strategy is about how your firm will present itself, and its products, in the host market. What determines the correct choice of entry strategy is based on both firm-related and market-related characteristics. Once these have been assessed, your firm is faced with three entry options: exporting, partnerships, or foreign direct investment. The chapter discusses both the advantages and disadvantages of each. The chapter also goes into the requirements for making each of these entry strategies successful.

7

Creating a Value Chain: Connecting with Your Customer

INTRODUCTION

Addressing the issue of creating a supply chain and dealing with logistics is a key element in our discussion of constructing a successful international business strategy. Too often this discussion tends to focus heavily on how to deal with the logistics of moving product and related materials across markets. While it is undeniable that the scope of the global marketplace represents a significant logistical challenge, there is much more to an effective supply chain than coordinating the physical movement of product, inputs, and other assets between market borders. The real purpose of a supply chain is to establish and maintain a connection with your customer. This is where the concept of a "value chain" enters the equation. In this chapter we will get into issues related to international logistics. However, our approach will be in the context of a supply chain that both delivers value to the customer and represents the conduit by which your firm can retain those customers through an ongoing relationship with your customer base.

The concept of a supply chain, or as we will refer to it a "value chain," encompasses the distribution channel that defines logistical activities as well as those very logistical activities that tie the distribution channel together. But that is only one piece of the puzzle. The value chain is all activities required to create and deliver a product into the hands of a customer. That means the value chain reaches back as far as the raw materials, components, and subassemblies that might go into the manufacture of a product and then extends from the product manufacturer to the wholesalers, dealers, retailers, and finally the ultimate end-user: your customer. Further, it also includes the logistical activities, or physical movement, of all associated resources that represent the linkages between these various stops in the chain. Thus, the value chain is the various pieces that make up the process of creating the product and putting it in the customer's hands and logistics are the activities that link these components of the chain.

To truly understand this concept of a value chain we need to consider how the members of the chain interact. This is value chain management—that is, the coordination of the value chain and its logistical activities. In order to have a functional value chain we must understand what the customer components of the chain want from the chain's members. Obviously the ultimate customer is the end-user of the product. But in order to maximize the efficiency of the value chain we must accept that any chain member "downstream," that is, any member that stands between your firm and the final customer becomes a customer in the value chain. So the question becomes: what do these customers want from the most immediate upstream member of the value chain? The final customer seeks product availability and service from the retailer, the retailer seeks inventory reliability among other things from the distributor, the distributor seeks a quality product from the manufacturer, and so on.

In turn, those members of the chain that interact with each of their "customers" placed downstream also have requirements they ask of these customers in order to keep the chain fully functional. The manufacturer expects the distributor to move its product without damaging it, the distributor expects the retailer to market the product effectively, and the retailer expects the final customer not to misuse the product. Inherent in all of these interactions is the purpose behind the value chain—to coordinate all of the members and their activities within your firm's business model through the physical implementation of your marketing strategy.

THE GLOBAL BUYING MARKET: UNDERSTANDING YOUR CUSTOMER

As the purpose of your value chain is to establish and maintain a connection with your customer we should take time to consider who your customer is—not in terms of demographics and creating a profile but rather in terms of understanding both what he seeks in your product and the means by which your firm can best create a connection with him. Your customer can be an end-user consumer, a business that uses your product in the course of conducting its own business, or increasingly U.S. firms are discovering that other governments can also be very attractive customers.

As we discussed in an earlier chapter, all end-user consumers seek to maximize product, service, personnel, and/or image value from your firm. At the same time they also seek to minimize their costs whether these are monetary/

financial, time, energy, or psychic. This is true of all individual consumers. Add in the additional complication of the importance of culture in understanding individual consumer behavior in international markets and the challenge of constructing an efficient value chain becomes substantial. For your international customers to be able to place your product where they will receive maximum value, at a time when they are most likely to seek out this value, we should take into account some of the areas of consumer behavior where your international customers may differ from those in your domestic market.

Putting "Value" in the International Value Chain

In understanding your international customer the best place to start is with the basic value she seeks out in your product; that is, what are the relevant buying motivations of your customer? People purchase automobiles to provide them with transportation. They also purchase cars to provide them with a feeling of independence as well as a sense of prestige. These are three different buying motivations and, depending upon which is most relevant, require different types and levels of service in the value chain. The customer who purchases a car for basic transportation will expect to be provided with basic transportation (e.g., a shuttle bus) when the car is in for service. On the other hand, the customer who purchases a car with the expectation of a feeling of independence will require a loaner car and the customer who places a high value on prestige in the car she drives will not accept just any loaner car—a Lexus owner will not be pleased with a Kia as a temporary substitute. These are similar yet different levels of service that must be executed within the value chain.

Above is an example of the value chain providing sought-for aspects of the overall product. The value chain must also be able to provide the product in a timely manner in the amounts sought for by the customer. This means that your firm, in order to establish an effective value chain, must have a clear understanding of the characteristics of your customers' buying behavior patterns. Questions like how often do your customers purchase the product and how much they purchase each time have important significance for your value chain. Consumers in Japan generally eat rice three times per day while consumers in the United States eat rice only about two to three times per month. The Japanese consumers eat rice in their homes and in restaurants while the U.S. consumer is more likely to eat rice at a restaurant. Thus, the value chain for rice in Japan must extend to both individual and institutional buyers and provide the product in much larger amounts (e.g., 25–50 lb. bags) while in the United States the value chain deals in smaller quantities both in packaging and in amount purchased.

Individual Consumers in International Markets

Moving beyond your product itself, any value chain strategy must also make allowances for what can be referred to as the "buying dynamic." The concept of the buying dynamic recognizes that products are often not evaluated, purchased, and used by just one single consumer. Instead, the consumption of many products takes place across more than one consumer. Your firm should consider the extent to which your product might create conflict within this buying dynamic. For example, breakfast cereal is not an inherently controversial product. At the same time, which breakfast cereals are considered for purchase and which are actually selected can involve inputs from both parents and children—a potential source of conflict between the healthy alternative and the choice that is associated with a cartoon character. By extension there is also the need to understand what characterizes the decision-making process for your product. In order to fully utilize all the value chain has to offer in managing your firm's relationship with its customers you need to have a clear picture as to who influences the purchase of your product, who makes the actual purchase, and who uses the product once it has been purchased.

Last, there is the issue of the mechanics of consumer behavior as these relate to connecting with your customer through the value chain. Because it is your connection to your customers, the value chain is often expected to perform promotional tasks. This means your firm must have some knowledge as to what your customer's expectations are regarding the promotion of your product as well as knowing enough about your customer's behavior to avoid alienating him with your message. It is not just about creating the "right" message—although that is important—it is also about the timing of the message. Just like the product itself must be available in the right place at the right time so too must the message that causes the consumer to seek out the product. This leads us to the issue that ties individual consumer behavior to value chain strategy. Possibly the single most important task that the value chain can perform is ensuring the product is actually in the right place at the right time. This means knowing exactly where your international customers expect to see your product and what other types of products they associate with yours. Consumers in the United States associate diapers with other regular consumption products such as those found in grocery stores. Japanese consumers, on the other hand, consider baby products to be "special care items" and tend to look for diapers and other baby products in a pharmacy.

Businesses as Customers

If your primary customer is a business, much of the conversation thus far related to individual customers becomes less relevant. Business customers differ from individual end-users in several ways. First, because your product is being purchased in order to further your business customer's own business, culture—particularly as it relates to tastes and preferences—is no longer a predominant issue as it is with individual customers. Further, those firms who target businesses rather than end-users often find that there are more international markets available to them. It is not uncommon for a market— especially emerging markets—to have little sustainable market demand for consumer products but these markets, as a result of their move to "emerge" as developed, can have sustainable demand from the business sector. Thus, firms with products targeted at businesses often find that in addition to developed markets they have substantial opportunities in these emerging markets as well. Another advantage to targeting business customers is that the transactions that take place between your firm and your customer firm can go beyond the traditional cash-for-product scenario through the utilization of countertrade.

A direct type of value chain, where the firm providing the product to businesses performs all the necessary activities of a value chain using countertrade as the basis for its market transaction, can reap significant advantages in international markets. Countertrade involves transactions where the actual money component of the transaction represents only partial payment. Businesses, unlike individual consumers, produce marketable products themselves on a relatively large scale. This means that the value that can be exchanged in a market transaction can potentially go beyond some form of cash payment. The biggest advantage to this approach to transactions, provided your firm can perform the required tasks of the value chain, is that you are now able to overcome the difficulties associated with credit and/or debt. No longer does your firm have to assume the risk credit and debt represent—through countertrade it can receive assets other than cash meaning that payment can be received much quicker and without the risk of default. This willingness to accept something other than currency in payment frequently means that other risks, like political risk, can be reduced in your market of choice, which also helps to facilitate market entry.

However, a direct value chain built on countertrade is not without disadvantages. There is the obvious problem associated with liquidity. It is one thing to accept partial payment in product; it is something else entirely to turn physical assets into actual currency. These countertrade deals can also be incredibly complex to execute—with a wide range of issues to be addressed such as the timing of ownership, how to account for damage to product on both sides of the transaction, storing, shipping, and a myriad of other details. In the end it is also difficult to determine how to price product in the transaction and the actual profit and/or loss that results from the transaction. How does a firm compare, for pricing and revenue purposes, the value over time of a durable good such as a computer to a nondurable good such as produce? It is tempting when dealing with business customers to create an internal value chain but like exporting, your firm must be able to perform all the necessary tasks of a value chain.

Governments as Customers

One customer type that requires a very unique value chain that is emerging in international business is that of governments. In areas outside of defense, U.S. government expenditures are shrinking but the increase in emerging markets based on their increased levels of economic development means that these markets are more attractive than they were previously. This increase in global development, and its subsequent increase in demand on the part of governments for a wide range of products, means that these governments are very attractive customers. Also, the size of the transactions cannot be overlooked—government contracts can be huge! Where is the impact on value chain strategy? When dealing with governments the value chain is almost always completely controlled within the firm. The reason is simple—when the size of government purchases is combined with the fact that there are a limited number of these customers, there is little need for creating an external value chain.

Now that we have addressed the issue of understanding your customer and how the value chain may, or may not, be able to assist your firm in establishing a long-term presence in a market we turn to how the value chain should function.

THE ROLE OF INFORMATION IN THE INTERNATIONAL VALUE CHAIN

The value chain is uniquely suited to assist your firm in achieving maximum effectiveness in your international operations. A well-managed value chain establishes that ongoing connection that assures your firm of a long-term steady flow of product to your customer we alluded to above—one that we will go into deeper as the chapter progresses. However, before we can enter into any further discussion of the specifics of value chain strategy, it is important we consider all the value chain has to offer. Understanding how to leverage the information that is a natural result of the interactions that take place up and down the value chain is a vital piece of value chain management.

This information has two fundamental uses. It can be used to gain information regarding the market in which your firm operates—information that is vital to not only success in that market but that may otherwise be difficult for your firm to obtain and that can be used to both fine tune existing strategies as well as assist in formulating improved market strategies in the future. Value chain information can also be employed to improve your firm's efficiencies in the ways it operates on a day-to-day basis in its international market, or markets. One of the keys to success in an international market lies with your company's ability to initiate and maintain interactions—it establishes connections in that market. By its very nature, the operation of your value chain creates these interactions and the information those interactions produce represent an invaluable asset in understanding the nuances of your international market.

Let's consider how just the day-to-day activities that are undertaken within a value chain can be employed to gather valuable market information. Many times important information regarding a market can be obtained by simply leveraging the logistical activities within the chain. For example, the use of real-time inventory tracking not only ensures a steady flow of product up and down the chain it also enables each member of the chain to be able to anticipate demand for your product—enabling your firm to be better able to meet the needs of your product's end-users. In other words, good management of your international value chain means not just maintaining product movement but learning as much as possible about this potentially unfamiliar market by systematically gathering and analyzing information related to all aspects of product movement—especially different aspects of product demand—throughout the entire value chain.

A further natural advantage of leveraging the information that is a by-product of these logistical activities is the ability of your firm to then reduce logistical costs. Over the years the concept of "just-in-time" inventory management has been put forth as a means by which firms can increase value chain efficiencies. Much of that discussion has been directed at manufacturers and their upstream suppliers (e.g., those firms supplying raw materials, components, and subassemblies to the firm producing a product). Being able to achieve that level of inventory control in the manufacturing process represents a tremendous efficiency. However, this "right place, right time" concept can also be applied to every step in the value chain all the way down to your product's final user. The costs associated with inventory stocking are always a problem in any value chain—domestic or international. These costs become critical in your international markets primarily because your firm is trying to balance the problem of reducing the costs associated with stocking products for which there may be no immediate demand with the potential costs associated with stocking out of product and the subsequent possibility that customers will turn to a substitute product—and not return to yours. The information available to your firm related to product movement can help to address both of these problems and enable you to minimize any excess product inventory while avoiding the danger of not having sufficient product available to meet customer demands.

The active analysis of value chain information can be also be used to make direct improvements in your firm's international market operations. Having a thorough understanding of your customer's product demand patterns can go far in improving all aspects of customer service such as knowing both when and what type of service is likely to be needed as well as service dependability, initiating interactive communication with your customers, and providing convenient service to these customers. The information can also be used to improve your firm's response to changing market demands as they relate to maintaining a close connection with your customer. For example, market information obtained through the value chain can assist your firm in staying relevant by providing the services that might be in demand as a result of changes in the market. Finally, value chain information can be used to improve your firm's response to changes in customer expectations such as how they obtain the product (e.g., the increased global popularity of online shopping in place of retail outlets). The lesson for us is this: given the time, effort, and variety of other resources that must be deployed to create an effective value chain it is almost a requirement that the chain be used to maximum benefit and that means leveraging the information it provides.

WHAT MAKES AN INTERNATIONAL VALUE CHAIN UNIQUE?

Moving your product to the final customer—be it individuals, businesses, or governments—represents a whole set of unique challenges when your firm moves from the known quantity of your domestic market into the international realm. Typically speaking, international distribution of your product is different in three ways. First, your value chain in international operations increases in length. The length of a value chain can be measured in terms of the number of members in the chain as well as in the actual distance between each member of the chain. In your international value chain the number of members generally increases particularly if any part of your international operations involves some form of import/exporting—either of the final product or the resources necessary to produce the final product. This means that managing relationships between the various members can become problematic as can your product pricing and positioning strategy because there is more pressure across the entire chain for each member to receive sufficient revenue from carrying your product. The physical length of the chain also increases in international operations. The physical distance has the potential to increase given the geographic distances between manufacturer and final customer; the number of chain members goes up along with the distance between the product manufacturer and the final customer. This increase in physical distance creates the possibility of a wide range of problems such as risk to the viability of the product as it moves across these greater distances.

A second way the international value chain is unique from your domestic chain is the decreased level of control your firm might be able to exert in its international markets. U.S. companies in particular are used to managing distribution through the application of power and influence. Manufacturers will attempt to control their value chain members through the active management of available inventory. Retailers will attempt to control manufacturers and other distributors through the power they hold in their access to customers. Unfortunately, in international markets your firm is likely to be more dependent upon the downstream members of the value chain than they are dependent on your firm.

A very common scenario is when the members of an established value chain in another market agree to accept a new nondomestic product. This product represents only a small portion of their overall business and requires that existing resources be applied—possibly to the detriment of established profitable products. In this situation, your firm's ability to exercise any power within the value chain is greatly reduced. At the end of the day, your firm needs the chain member's ability to move product to its final customer destination more than the chain needs your product. This can mean that your firm and product could be placed in a less than ideal situation—one that could have been avoided if there was more control exerted by your firm in the value chain. A German manufacturer of indoor space heaters learned this lesson the hard way in Taiwan. Indoor space heaters are very popular in Asian markets where many homes lack central heating. With a clear demand opportunity in Taiwan, the firm in question employed a local distributor to market and sell its products. The Taiwanese distributor chose to use the promotional tagline "Declare War on the Cold Front" along with an image of Adolf Hitler in its marketing and sales campaign. Understandably, the German manufacturer was displeased by the campaign but could do little as the Taiwanese firm was its only means of connecting with the customer in that lucrative market and in an effort to reduce risk, the German company had transferred ownership of the product units to its Taiwanese distributor immediately when the products arrived in Taiwan.

The third area where the international value chain tends to be uniquely different from that in your domestic market is in the area of structure. U.S. firms are in a singularly unique market when it comes to value chain strategy and distribution of product. The market in the United States is both large in number of customers and in geographic area. This means that in the United States there are a number of substantial regional markets spread across the country. This, in turn, means there is an entire layer of regional members within the value chain. International markets are much less likely to have this large regional value chain structure; rather, the downstream value chain in international markets is more likely to be on either end of a spectrum—either full of a large number of smaller members or dominated market-wide by a small number of very large members. There are advantages and disadvantages to each type of structure. In the case of many small members, the firm with the product is more likely to be able to exert power over its distributors but at the expense of having to manage the logistics and relationships that go along with a large number of chain members. On the other hand, in the situation where there are a very limited number of chain members, your firm's ability to exert power may be minimal but having only a very small number of chain members to deal with—who can provide wide access to the market—may be attractive.

INTERNATIONAL VALUE CHAIN STRATEGY

Taking into account these unique features of the international value chain, let's consider the foundation of an international value chain. These pieces—commonly referred to as the six Cs of international value chain strategy—are cost, capital, control, coverage, character, and continuity. By focusing your efforts in putting together an effective and efficient value chain strategy built on these six elements you and your firm are more likely to obtain positive long-term results.

Taking into account the numerous tasks that must be performed by the value chain the issue of high start-up costs is a given. What is frequently overlooked, however, is that these start-up costs are just that—the necessary investment to establish the value chain. U.S. firms commonly neglect to sufficiently plan for the costs associated with maintaining the chain. The role of the value chain is to establish and *maintain* a connection with your customers. Your value chain strategy must plan for the ongoing maintenance of the chain. This naturally leads to the second C—capital. Because your value chain comprises multiple members it is important to not only consider how much capital will be required but also how this capital provision will be spread across the chain members. We have alluded to the challenges of control within the value chain—a well-developed international value chain strategy explicitly decides how your firm will manage the members of the chain and how control will be exerted. Coverage involves determining how much of your product will be made available in the market and where (i.e., the type of outlet) it will be made available. The last two Cs—character and continuity—deal with the nature of the chain (e.g., direct vs. indirect) and the need to build stability into your international value chain.

International Value Chain Options

Using these six Cs as a guide for creating an international value chain, the question now turns to making the choice between a direct chain and an indirect chain. Direct distribution offers the potential for a higher level of control within your international market along with greater potential profits and closer direct contact with your customers. However, the resource commitment—both in time and money—causes many firms to choose an indirect approach instead. Much like indirect exporting as a market entry strategy, an indirect value chain enables your firm to get its product to the customer with a much lower level of resource commitment. Again, like indirect exporting, the indirect value chain uses host market entities to place your product in the hand of your customers.

One means of indirect distribution would be the use of some type of commission agent. As the name suggests, these individuals work on commission and often actively seek out products to fill the need of a client—many times the client being a government agency. The real advantage to utilizing a commission agent is that he does not get paid until the product is actually purchased. However, not all types of products lend themselves well to being circulated within a market through these commission agents. An alternative, which also represents a very low level of resource commitment, would be an export agent or remarketer. Like the commission agent, an export agent is highly motivated to move your product—but his underlying motivation is somewhat different. A commission agent only gets paid if the product sells, but does not actually take title to the product. The export agent, on the other hand, will purchase your product and then remarket the product in the host market. The advantage is apparent—any problems in managing the value chain are out of the hands of your firm and placed squarely upon the export agent. The difficulty here is one of control. The export agent owns the product so in principle he can market your product any way he sees fit—a problem already highlighted with the German heater example.

For firms desiring a more active, long-term role in their international value chain, while retaining the primary advantage of an indirect approach, there are also the options of engaging an export management or trading company or the alternative of utilizing a "piggyback" marketing approach. Both the export management and trading companies act essentially as distribution departments for a number of outside firms whose products tend to be noncompeting. These firms have the significant advantage of being well established in your host market—their business is exactly what a value chain is supposed to be, a sustained connection with customers. This is very often the avenue of choice for firms trying to establish an effective value chain in a short period of time.

"Piggyback" marketing has a similar attraction but works somewhat differently. In this type of arrangement another firm "adopts" your product in order to round out its own product line. This is a good choice particularly if your firm has a limited product line, or the target market is relatively small. Firms in this position can conclude that international markets simply do not represent a sufficiently large opportunity relative to the resources that would have to be invested in order to be successful. By utilizing a piggyback approach the firm can overcome the problem of resource commitment and at the same time make its product more attractive in the market by having it paired with other complementary products. A small Wisconsin firm was able to use piggyback marketing in placing its vinyl windows in Northern Europe. A large building supply firm in that market had a gap in its product line when it came to replacement windows. By supplying its vinyl windows to this larger, local firm the U.S. company not only avoided having to create its own value chain but it avoided the challenge of having to create market awareness and interest for what is a product with limited natural appeal.

Constructing an International Value Chain

Regardless of the means by which your firm chooses to create an indirect value chain, there are compelling advantages to this approach. Apart from the cost and resource savings already pointed out, the members of the indirect chain have invaluable knowledge of the host market, the ability to quickly identify and track the competition, and can reduce any possible language and other cultural difficulties. These are all serious reasons for choosing to connect with your customer through an indirect value chain. So what criteria should be used when selecting members of your chain?

Because these members of the value chain have the responsibility to channel your product to the customers a good place to start in the process of selecting members would be with what are known as "product factors." These relate to any special skills or knowledge a potential member might possess from which your product would benefit. For example, do they deal with complementary products that would enhance your product offering? Do they have a high level of recognition in the market? Are they able to provide unique benefits such as intellectual property or brand protection? Anything that could serve to more effectively and efficiently establish your product in the host market would be considered a product factor. Extending this concept of product factors, a second area to assess would be marketing skills. How well is the member likely to be able to establish and maintain the relationships required of her in her stage of the value chain? Can she adequately assist in the promotion of your product? If necessary can she provide the appropriate level of service? The goal in assessing potential members from the perspective of product factors and marketing skills is to go directly to the heart of what a value chain is supposed to provide—the members' ability individually and collectively to connect with the customer.

Moving beyond their potential in performing fundamental responsibilities, you should also assess areas related to the long-term viability of the chain. Do the chain and its members possess what is sometimes referred to as "facilitating factors" such as political connections? What is their financial and overall corporate position (e.g., credit rating, ability to handle growth)? How committed are they? The issue of commitment, and increasing that commitment, is at the heart of the long-term viability of your value chain. The higher the levels of commitment, the more the chain is likely to be viable over time.

Commitment can be a tricky area to evaluate—especially if your firm is not in a position to, or cannot, require large financial investment from your host chain members. But that is not to say that it cannot be assessed. A practical means of assessing commitment is through either current, or anticipated, product participation. This is a basic three-step commitment model. When one or more members of your value chain is willing to share the costs of promoting your product to the next downstream participant—or even all the way down to your final customer—that is generally taken to represent the first major step in obtaining commitment. Step two would be when these same member, or members, agree to take on significant inventory levels—a cost generally avoided by host market members if your product does not represent what they believe to be substantial revenue opportunity. Step three is when these members agree to give your product preference over the competition—or ideally carry your product to the exclusion of any potential competing products.

RELEVANT ISSUES IN CONSTRUCTING AN INTERNATIONAL VALUE CHAIN

We have established the framework and areas that must be addressed in order to create an effective value chain in your international market. At this point it would also be helpful to consider some relevant issues that could impact your value chain strategy and the likelihood of its success.

The first set of these issues includes those that pertain to the functioning of each member. The most important of these are "middlemen" services, line breadth, and costs and margins. In the case of middlemen services it is easy to assume that the way each member of the value chain functions in your international market will be the same as your home market. In the United States especially downstream chain members are expected to provide some aspect of customer service such as accepting product returns, providing product replacements, servicing products, even jointly paying for advertising and promotion. These activities cannot be taken for granted in your host market. Firms that tend to be most successful have only the most basic initial expectations of their value chain members—provision of physical transportation of the product. By adopting this perspective they force themselves to gain a clear understanding of all the functions that must be performed in the chain and, if experience shows these activities can be performed by the chain members, they have a knowledge base from which to implement a change. Assuming that any middlemen services will automatically be performed in the host market leaves your firm open to the very real threat that they simply won't be performed.

The issues of line breadth and costs and margins among the chain members have to do with the role of your product from the viewpoint of the members. Line breadth refers to the product line your value chain members carry. As pointed out above, in an ideal situation—with a high level of member commitment—your product would be given preference, maybe even exclusivity, in the member's product line. Reality shows, however, that this level of commitment is very difficult to obtain and takes time—if it can ever be reached at all. It is more likely that your product will be more or less equally placed within the member's product line. It is the responsibility of your firm to actively evaluate what potentially competing products also exist in the product line and your product's role in the overall product line. Your objective is for your product to take a primary, not secondary or support role, in the product line. Last, the issue of costs and margins is one where your firm must consider if there is an accepted norm for revenue-impacting areas such as product mark-up for chain members and where the control typically lies in the administration of these costs.

Moving to the relevant issues of the connections between the chain members, we must consider the actual length of the chain that is required in the host market along with the concept of the value chain held by customers in that market. When it comes to chain length it is difficult to come up with any hard-and-fast rules that apply to all markets, but there are general guidelines based on your product and the type of market. Typically, more developed markets have longer value chains than those in emerging or lesser developed markets. This is due to a couple of factors; first, developed markets are more likely to have a larger number of viable target market segments. Second, the customers sold product in developed markets often expect high levels of customer service and product support, which requires a certain amount of specialization on the part of the chain members leading to a longer overall value chain. On the other hand, premium-priced specialty consumer products—such as watches—will employ as short a value chain as possible in order to maintain a high level of control over their product's performance in the marketplace. In the case of industrial—or business-to-business—products the relatively smaller number of total customers, the tailored marketing approach that is often necessary, and the high level of service and support expectations cause these channels to be relatively short.

This brings us then to the two most common relevant issues—or in this case problem areas—that are encountered in establishing and maintaining an international value chain. These are "blocked" channels and the high cost of stocking/inventory. A "blocked" channel occurs when a local competitor attempts to exert control over the value chain in order to prevent your product from utilizing the chain and ultimately gaining access to customers. About a decade ago the Ford Motor Company embarked on a plan to open up 200 new independent dealerships per year in Japan over a five-year period of time. At the end of that five-year time frame it had achieved a total of 35—all company-owned.

The failure to achieve the stated goals was a blocked channel. Ford had assumed that, as was the case with its firm and the willingness to work with Toyota in the United States, Ford automobiles would be seen as complementing the cars sold by Japanese dealers. The Japanese manufacturers did not see the situation the same—they viewed Ford as a real potential rival and set about trying to prevent Ford from accessing customers. Exerting its power over the dealers, Toyota simply threatened to cut off cooperative promotional activities, training of service and technical personnel, spare parts, and ultimately inventory. These independent dealers were not willing to risk everything in their established businesses on a new American car line. The result was a very effectively blocked channel—destroying the value chain before it could even be constructed.

The problem associated with the high cost of stocking, on the other hand, is not one where your firm and its product are denied access to the customer but rather where the burden of ensuring a steady flow of product through the chain falls primarily to your firm. Value chain members tend to avoid the costs associated with large inventories and many of the attending issues such as high credit costs, currency exchange issues, inflation, and so forth. The result is that it may fall to your firm to employ its own quasi-JIT (just-in-time) supply system for some, possibly all, members of your value chain, placing not only a huge direct cost burden on the chain but the attending logistical headaches as well. What, then, can we look for in trying to identify solid long-term members in our international value chain?

KEYS TO SUCCESS WHEN DEALING WITH INTERNATIONAL VALUE CHAIN MEMBERS

In many ways what your firm should seek out in dealing with your international value chain members is very similar to what you might look for if your firm chooses some form of partnership in your market entry strategy. Each member of your value chain is, in effect, a partner. Therefore, your chain is most effectively managed through a relational approach. The best place to begin is with ensuring a high level of formalization between your firm and the other members—in other words, make sure that the responsibilities of every member are explicitly established. Within that formalized structure three areas need to be addressed. These are reciprocity, intensity, and conflict.

The goal of reciprocity is to ensure that there is a high degree of mutual decision making within the chain. That is not to say that your international value chain has to be a democracy with all members having equal influence—such a situation would be counterproductive to the purpose of managing the chain. However, in order to achieve maximum effectiveness throughout the chain, the notion of mutual decision making will help your firm to leverage the information available through the value chain and, at the same time, ensure a higher level of "buy-in" from the chain members for any decisions that are made. Intensity refers to mutual resource commitment. As we have established, mutual resource commitment does not mean equal proportions of the same inputs. That would defeat the purpose of the chain—where each member brings some unique value to the overall structure. Instead, mutual resource commitment is designed to ensure that each member fills a unique role while also ensuring the necessary mutual dependencies that will assist in the long-term functionality of the value chain. Last is the need to address the issue of conflict. Again, like a partnership-based market entry strategy, your international value chain will function best over time if conflict is avoided in favor of relationally based member interaction.

SUMMARY

This chapter was devoted to understanding the many facets of international value chain creation and implementation. While the discussion addressed the relevant points related to an international supply chain, it expanded the concept to encompass all the activities that must be taken into consideration in order to effectively reach customers—and maintain that relationship over time. The notion of "value" was contextualized from the perspective of the three major customer groups—individuals, businesses, and governments. The role of information in value chain strategy was highlighted along with the unique aspects of an international value chain. The discussion then moved to international value chain strategy, its underlying components, how to construct an international value chain, the common problems that are encountered in international value chain construction and management, and finally, the keys to success in dealing with the various members of your international value chain.

PART III

GOING INTERNATIONAL

8

Making Your Business Viable: Creating an International Product Strategy

INTRODUCTION

At the heart of your international operations is your firm's product strategy. Up to this point, in many ways, we have focused our attention on ensuring you and your firm were ready to take the big step into international business. Our discussion has gone from understanding how to deal with the various facets of the international business environment to issues such as how to assess potential markets, how to enter those markets, and the challenges of reaching your customer. All of this represents what could be characterized as "setting the stage." At this juncture we should have a clear grasp of what it takes to move from thinking about international operations to actually operating internationally. The missing pieces represent the foundation of your international business model—the product and how to present that product to the market. In this chapter and the next we are going to deal with each of these pieces. In this chapter we will look at the various issues relevant to developing an international product strategy and in the next how to communicate the existence and importance of that product offering to your international market, or markets.

International product strategy can be best addressed by considering three product-related issues. The first, product concept determination, deals with the assessment of your product in the context of your international market. That is, what is the value your new customers will seek out, and ultimately receive, from your product? What these international customers seek from your firm and its product can often be very different from those in your home market. McDonald's customers in China pay a premium to eat at McDonald's for the "cultural experience"—not a product positioning strategy that is likely to be attractive here in the United States. Second, your firm must consider aspects of product design strategy. The key question here is the extent to which your product might need to be customized, or adapted, for your new market(s). Third, and finally, there are the different areas (e.g., branding, packaging) related to product management that must be taken into consideration. These three issue categories represent our map for the discussion of international product strategy.

PRODUCT CONCEPT DETERMINATION

Product strategy extends far beyond simply ascertaining features to include, or exclude, on a tangible good. Many companies have a significant service component to their product offering while others deal solely with a service-based product. It is important at the outset that we understand what represents a product before we embark on our discussion of product strategy. Simply put, a product is *all* of both the tangible and intangible values a customer receives when purchasing and using that product. This would apply to the features and functionality of a tangible good, but also to aspects of the product such as where the product is available—Blockbuster Video is a poster child for location value having watched its market share in the United States erode almost overnight as companies like Netflix and Red Box have made videos easier to obtain. There are also intangible aspects of the product such as brand equity, service, product image, and so forth. Your product is everything a customer receives from your firm, which means to develop an effective international product strategy your firm must be able to fully grasp *everything* your international customers will both seek out and receive when they purchase your product.

The fundamental key to success in your international product strategy is to be able to correctly identify the "satisfactions" a customer receives from your product and then, by extension, determine whether or not these change from market to market. For example, the satisfactions a customer could potentially receive from purchasing and consuming a soft drink might be thirst-quenching, an energy boost, or the soda may be a health-conscious alternative drink choice. This is borne out by the various promotional campaigns that present the satisfaction, or value proposition, customers seek. The thirst-quenching value set would be Sprite ("Obey Your Thirst"), energy boost Mountain Dew ("Do the Dew"), and health conscious Diet Coke ("Zero Calories and All the Flavor").

All of these product value sets work well in the United States, but many do not translate to other markets. Outside the United States, Sprite is often presented as an alternative to traditional cola products; Mountain Dew is not widely sold outside of the United States as the energy drink category was long established with other non-U.S. products such as Red Bull; and as for Diet Coke, Coke has discovered over the years that many international consumer segments do not define a health product by what is missing but rather by what extra or healthy ingredients are actually in the product. In order to effectively evaluate exactly what your international customer expects from your product you and your firm must be able to think outside of the box in terms of what values your product represents. This is not a discussion of what product category your offering belongs in—quite the contrary. This discussion is about what possible values and uses your product could provide to a potential customer regardless of the product category it fits into in its home market.

Your product comprises three basic components: the actual product core, its brand and package, and its auxiliary or support services. In conducting your product concept determination a review of the actual product core really boils down to answering two questions: why is it purchased and how can it be used? A popular car wash product in the United States is marketed and sold in the car care section of major retailers. The exact same product is sold at retailers specializing in lawn care and landscaping products in Japan and in major home improvement stores in the Netherlands. The physical product itself does not change, but in the United States it is used to wash cars, in Japan it is used to wash bamboo—commonly used in landscaping—and in the Netherlands it is used to wash homes. The same product but very different value propositions. Similarly, the role and purpose of your brand and package—which we will discuss in more detail later—may be very different in your international market. To borrow from an example in an earlier chapter, Foster's Lager has little brand equity in its home market but represents a premium brand in its international markets. Further, its unique 25 oz. can was conceived to meet the demands of the more-bang-for-your-buck Australian target market but is used in its international markets as a distinguishing feature. The auxiliary or support services we have touched on, most notably in the value chain discussion, but it is important that we remember that the customer does not distinguish between tangible and intangible aspects of the product. Everything these customers receive from your firm becomes some aspect of the product offering and it is incumbent upon your firm to be able to not only provide a relevant core product but also all the other product elements these new customers expect.

PRODUCT DESIGN STRATEGY

Perhaps the biggest consideration in international product strategy is dealing with the issue of the extent to which your product—all facets of your product—needs to be customized, or somehow adapted for your new market(s). Given the resource commitments associated with any product change, the goal of firms is to try and present as standardized a product offering as possible in all markets in which they operate. However, as your product offering represents all value components sought by your customer, and that every market is to some extent different from your home market, the possibility that some level of customization will be necessary is very real.

Product Standardization versus Product Customization

Because your product is the bundle of values received by your customer, the most logical place to start in determining if any type of product customization needs to take place is with the nature of the product and its customers. Certain categories of products are more likely to need to be adapted for a local market than others. In general, products with individual consumers as the end-user require more customization than business-to-business or industrial products. Taking into account the typical types of consumer products a large proportion have a value proposition in which individual tastes and preferences define the bundle of values. Food, clothing, and a myriad of other products targeted at individuals are differentiated along the line of various aspects of tastes and preferences. Add in the cultural component and the need to somehow adapt the product to consumers in each market becomes compelling. Business-to-business or industrial products, on the other hand, do not require much in the way of customization because the product is being used internally for the purpose of producing the customer's product.

Having said that products targeted at individual customers require customization it is important to point out that not all products require the same attention—durable products can often be standardized across different consumer markets due to the very nature of these products. Where nondurable products such as food and clothing are highly influenced by individual tastes, preferences, and cultural differences the value propositions associated with durable products is likely to have more to do with the functionality of the product. Products like automobiles and household appliances are purchased with an eye toward what they do—not always just what they might represent. This means that the adaptation of these products can be done in ways that are less cost-heavy. Changing the color on a car or a refrigerator is much less expensive than changing the fundamental product core itself. Thus, in the quest to minimize product customization—and maximize any possible economies of scale associated with a product standardized across multiple markets—the first area to consider is the extent to which your customer's individual tastes and preferences influence whether or not your product represents an attractive value bundle.

International Market Development and Product Strategy

The level of development of your international market, or markets, will also heavily influence the degree to which your firm may need to customize its product offering to each individual market. Here we are not referring to the economic development of these markets necessarily but rather to the experience these markets may, or may not, have with the type of product your firm has to offer. One of the reasons a firm will select a particular international market is because of the opportunity to operate within a market that has a lower level of competitive intensity. The lack of competing products in that market may mean your firm has the ability to grab market share relatively easily, but this lack of competition may also mean that your product is in a different stage of the product life cycle.

When your firm has decided to consider international operations because its product offering(s) are in the mature stage of the product life cycle in its current market the opportunity presented by a new market also means that your product is likely in an earlier stage of the product life cycle, which, in turn, may dictate that your firm make some alterations to your product strategy. One of the traditional ways a firm keeps its product relevant in a mature market is by introducing variations within the product line or adding new features. For example, Apple has maintained dominance in the MP3 music market in the United States through the introduction of more and more advanced iPod products. However, Apple—a firm that prides itself as being high-tech, gadget-oriented—has discovered that these products do not fare so well in the emerging markets it seeks to expand into. Rather than the most advanced touch screens and download capabilities, products like preloaded MP3 players with limited memory capacity make more sense in their new markets. An absence of necessary Internet access and capabilities combined with the newness of the product concept means that a preloaded iPod Shuffle with a few hundred songs is a much more viable product—but this same product variation has little appeal in Apple's established markets.

International Product Strategy and the Market Environment

This then leads us to the next area related to the market environment that may dictate how much your product might need to be adapted—the existence of a support system for your product. One of the areas related to product strategy and product adaptation that is easy for U.S. firms to overlook is the existence of the infrastructure necessary to make the product usable. Advanced technological products clearly need advanced infrastructure and support systems. However, many of the products that we take for granted in the United States require an advanced support system in order to be relevant.

For example, Lever Bros. is one of the largest frozen vegetable companies in the world. The attraction of frozen vegetables over the canned variety crosses cultures—frozen vegetables simply are closer to fresh in virtually all respects when compared to canned. The problem is simple—in order for frozen vegetables to be viable in a market that market needs the capability to keep the product frozen. That means uninterrupted electricity and for every member of the value chain—down to the individual consumer—to possess a freezer. In the absence of these two basic support elements, the product represents no value. That leaves Lever Bros. with two options: forego the markets without these support systems or somehow adapt the product. Lever Bros. has learned that freeze-dried, vacuum-sealed vegetables represent an acceptable product variation in markets that cannot support the frozen type. They can be stored for extended periods of time, the logistical problems and costs associated with canned vegetables are avoided, and upon preparation the freeze-dried vegetables compare more closely to frozen/fresh vegetables than products that are canned. While it is an easy area to overlook, not ensuring the existence of the necessary product support system within your international market can be a key contributor to the failure of any product strategy.

The physical environment, an area related to the existing support system in your market of choice, is another influencer on the extent to which your firm's product may need to be customized for your international market. Where the support system is associated with whether or not your market of choice has the infrastructure necessary to use your product in place and available for your customer, the issue identified with the physical environment deals with the impact the physical surroundings in the market might have on the viability of your product. This impact can come in the form of the climate and other natural characteristics of the physical environment or it can come in the form of man-made characteristics of the environment. In the context of the natural environment, computer firms targeting small businesses have found the Asian market to be very lucrative in terms of demand, but U.S. firms in the industry have also found that a high amount of airborne particulates exist in small businesses in Asia compared to those located in the United States requiring the products to be made more "dust resistant." At the same time, many man-made aspects of the environment—changes in electricity requirements, amount of storage space available to your customer, and so forth—can also demand your product be adapted to your new market(s).

It is not uncommon for firms to lean as far as possible toward standardizing their product. The high costs associated with product customization lead many firms to push the envelope when it comes to producing and marketing a single variation of product. Put quite simply, the cost-benefit relationship—when it comes to product customization—simply is not favorable. It is easy to see the benefits of product standardization—economies of scale, a consistent product offering and the attending consistencies in promotional strategy, more efficient production processes—the list is long. However, too much obvious standardization—especially when it is perceived by the consumers in your firm's host market as a compromise product offering—can result in less obvious opportunity costs such as ineffective market penetration and even outright resentment of your firm and its products. So, what might be some characteristics of products—particularly consumer products—that might lend themselves more easily to higher levels of standardization?

Characteristics of a "Standardizable" Product

Generally speaking, there are four basic characteristics of an easily standardized consumer product. Products that have all four are often more associated with well-established large firms, but not always. First, products with wide brand recognition are more likely to be easily standardized across markets. The logic is simple—products with some level of universal brand recognition are products that have an identity of their own. Thus, the universal brand recognition is part of a larger product characteristic—that is, the brand has universal recognition because the product has universal appeal (e.g., Coke). That is not to say that these products do not require some adaptation in certain markets—they are less likely than products with less universal appeal to need some level of customization. This relates to some degree to the second characteristic, which is the need for little, if any, product knowledge in order for the consumer to use the product. A product that is simple to use is one that often cannot be customized as there are few adaptation options. In the absence of product complexity there are not many alternative product variations that might be viable.

Where the first two characteristics of an easily standardized product are more related to the product itself, the second two are related to the market in which the product is sold. Products that require low information content in the promotional messages are also considered to be more easily standardized across different markets. These types of products can frequently be presented to the consumers in a market using visual communication tools—tools that require little or no changes between markets because the product value bundle is self-evident. Nivea Skin Cream can show its benefits simply through the portrayal of product use—application to the skin—with the resulting benefits also being obvious. Finally, when the market your firm is entering has a low or nonexistent negative country-of-origin effect there may be no need to make product alterations as the hidden opportunity costs that can be incurred when consumers in a market see your product as a "foreign" compromise do not exist.

PRODUCT MANAGEMENT STRATEGY

The prospect of managing the multitude of issues related to international product strategy could easily be seen to be a daunting task. However, the job becomes somewhat less intimidating if we stop and consider the key elements of product strategy that are critically important to your firm and its product(s) as you move into new markets outside your home base of operations. The critical areas of international product management strategy are product line strategy, brand management, packaging, and product service.

International Product Line Management

Product line management—particularly for firms new to international markets—focuses on how to deal with the potential problem of multiple products (which to introduce to the new market, which to omit for international operations, and the timing of the product line roll-out) as well as the adoption and diffusion of the product, or products. Firms with a single product in the product line do not have to address the challenge of managing the product line. However, few firms have only a single product—even the most basic of products has aspects that can be adapted or varied and these constitute a product line as the determination must be made as to which of these adaptations or variants will be available in the new market.

One way of looking at this issue is from the perspective of the firm with a product line clearly comprising multiple products. The firm in this situation must approach international product line management by directly dealing with the question of how best to extend that product line into the host market. This is a two-fold issue: first, the number of products in the line to be extended into the new host market, and second, the timing of the introduction of these products. Extending the home market product line can be a tricky endeavor. On one hand your firm does not want to incur all the resource costs associated with bringing a product into another market if that product is not going to produce sufficient revenue return—either because it does not represent value to the local customers or because it steals sales away from the other products in your firm's line. On the other hand, your firm does not want to leave money on the table by not introducing as large a product line as possible into your host market.

In order to effectively manage the international product line the problem can be boiled down to these two fundamental issues: what products will be relevant and when they should be introduced. In the case of the former, your firm needs to recognize the role each product plays in the product line—both as an independent product and in support of the other products in the line. The problem to avoid is one where there is no clear identity for one or more of the products in the line, which can result in confusion among your potential customers (i.e., they simply cannot see what makes the products distinct) along with steering clear of a situation where your firm's products "cannibalize" each other (i.e., "steal" sales from within your own product line rather than from the competition). With some products there may be a clear separation but with others—especially those in a well-developed, sophisticated product line—the differences may be less apparent particularly among consumers with little or no knowledge of the products (e.g., consumers in a market new to the product).

Assuming your firm has multiple product offerings within the same product line, and only those products deemed to be relevant in the new host market have been retained in the line, your firm must then plan for the introduction of each product into the new market. This is the process already referred to as "extending" your home market product line. The process is employed when your firm possesses at least one strong core brand and then, using incremental introduction of individual products, extends the product line in a gradual progression into your international market. Using Coca Cola as a hypothetical example, the process would look something like this: Coke (the original cola) would be introduced first, based on the strength of its brand worldwide. Next, the Sprite brand might be brought into the market as a thirst-quenching alternative soft drink—note: not as an alternative to the Coke brand, but a noncola soda as there is a clear distinction between those who prefer cola and noncola soft drinks. Then the fruit-based Fanta brand would be introduced and, finally, other variations such as the diet alternatives would be introduced to finish the process. All of this would take place over time with the goal of establishing a unique identity for each product while enabling the firm to maximize sales within the selected market.

Product Adoption and Diffusion in International Markets

Introducing one, or more, products into your firm's chosen market brings us to the other important aspect of product, or product line, management in international markets: that of the adoption and diffusion of new products within a market. While having a clear idea as to which of your firm's products represent a true value offering is a cornerstone for success, the speed at which the market may, or may not, accept that product is equally as important. It is generally accepted that in every market there are a small, but significant, number of consumers who are willing to take a chance on a new product. Known as "early adopters," reaching these individuals is the crucial first step in a successful product introduction. Once this group has accepted, or "adopted," the product the stage is set for this adoption to spread, or diffuse, to the other customers in the market. Having an understanding of this adoption and diffusion process is fundamentally important to product success as this understanding can be used to speed the process by identifying and leveraging those aspects of the process in which your firm's products have unique strengths.

The speed of the adoption and diffusion process is influenced by three categories of characteristics: product-related, market-related, and impact-related. The product-related characteristics are specific to your firm's product offering. Any of these characteristics that your firm's products possess will help to speed the adoption and diffusion process. At the same time, anything your firm can do to improve either the real, or perceived, nature of its product relative to these characteristics will also increase its rate of adoption and diffusion within a market.

Perhaps the most important of these product-related characteristics is your product's real, or what consumers perceive to be, relative advantage over substitute products. Apple's iPod MP3 player is an excellent example of a product with substantial relative advantage over alternative music/entertainment storage and delivery systems. These—indeed virtually all MP3 devices—have the capability to store and play literally thousands of songs and movies yet are the size of a mobile phone. When Apple combined this product advantage with its iTunes music/entertainment library and well-stocked store it meant the rapid decline of the CD music industry worldwide. The huge storage capacity, digital quality delivery, extremely compact size, and a purchase/file management system meant that the iPod had clear relative advantage over all alternative products, resulting in the iPod product line becoming the global standard for portable entertainment.

Looking at the other factors contributing to rapid product adoption and diffusion—compatibility, complexity, and communicability—the iPod also possesses these characteristics as well. For power and battery charge it uses the global standard USB plugs and Internet downloads, making it compatible with all Internet access points (i.e., computers) across the globe. The iPod has a low level of product complexity—it is very intuitive in terms of operation—also making it easy for consumers to adopt. Finally, it is easy to communicate its relative advantage—as demonstrated by Apple's visually based promotional messages, which are used in virtually every market. In order to speed your host market's acceptance of your new product offering, your firm must consciously emphasize not only the unique benefits of the product but also the ease of adopting the product—that is, the low level of switching costs. Products that can directly, and credibly, address these product characteristics are more likely to have a successful product introduction.

The adoption and diffusion process is not only influenced by product characteristics, however. The nature of your customers also will dictate the speed of the process. In an international market the extent to which your customer segments are willing to innovative—or take product risks—is a key factor as well. It is important to point out that consumer innovativeness is a characteristic of the customer's behavior in the market. It is not necessarily tied to cultural traits. Were that the case, it would be relatively easy to identify markets where consumers were predisposed toward new product adoption, and those where the process might be problematic. A more traditionally oriented market, such as Japan, would then be identified with a more conservative approach to consumption and be less inclined to adopt new products where a culturally eclectic market like the United States would be very open to new product adoption. The reality is the opposite: Japanese consumers are very willing and quick to try all types of new products where American consumers tend to be much more reluctant. Just as it is necessary to have a clear picture as to where your product fits in terms of its adoption and diffusion characteristics it is also crucial to have a good idea as to the receptivity of the consumers in your host market when it comes to new products.

Moving beyond the consumer's willingness to innovate and try new products, there are also the consumer behavior issues of need perception and economic ability to consider. Closely related to your product's relative advantage is the notion of need perception. Consumers in your international market, or markets, will only take the risk on your new product if they can perceive a clear need. By focusing much of your market communications on the product characteristics discussed above, a natural byproduct—assuming your firm makes a clear and credible case in those communications—would be an increase in the perceived need, on the part of consumers, for your product. The key word in all of this is *perceived*. The market, being composed of consumers, will act on what it thinks it knows—not necessarily on what might be considered objective truth. Thus, as your firm presents a compelling case for the advantages of its products and the ease of adopting that same product, the perception among consumers that they are missing something will rise. Combine this with the ability to purchase your product and the market would now be considered very favorable for a reasonably rapid new product adoption and diffusion process.

We are then left with one more group of characteristics to take into account—impact-related characteristics. These deal with the impact that the adoption of a new product will have on the market and the consumers in the market. The general rule-of-thumb is that the greater the impact a new product has on a market (i.e., the more the product requires the market and its consumers to change) the slower the adoption and diffusion process. In the 1980s when music format shifted from record albums to CDs it had a major impact on the music markets around the world. In a relatively short period of time firms in the market were forced to make major inventory changes as CDs became the standard format. At the same time, individual consumers also had to acquire the necessary electronics to play the CDs along with the actual CDs themselves—in many cases replacing their music libraries with the same music they owned on vinyl records. This would suggest a scenario for a long, drawn-out adoption and diffusion process. The reality was just the opposite. The record industry was estimating about a five-year adoption time frame due largely to the fact that consumers would be asked to make major changes and investments before they could be considered to be wholly committed to the new format. In truth the process took less than two years in the international market because of the overwhelming relative advantage of the product. That is the lesson: your firm should understand that new products will have some impact—more or less—on the market and its consumers. By leveraging the product characteristics—particularly the perceived relative advantage—your firm can effectively deal with these impact-related characteristics of a given market(s) and increase the speed of the adoption and diffusion process.

To this point we have dealt with the key challenges of managing your core product offering in an international setting. The other areas of international product strategy—branding, packaging, and warranties/service—could be considered to be "support" activities. However, if they are well managed, they can create a solid foundation to not only support but also enhance your overall product offering. A good starting point is with branding your product. Regardless of the characteristics of a given market, the best brand names are user-friendly (i.e., easy to pronounce), have a high recall level (i.e., easy to remember), and also have either an explicit or implied positive association with the product (e.g., Bold laundry detergent). The overall objective of the brand name is to create a label to distinctly identify the product—so that when consumers hear, see, or use the brand name they reflexively conjure up the entire bundle of values that constitute the product.

International Branding

These key features of a "good" brand name do not only apply in international markets—these are universal brand principles. At the same time, when your firm moves into new international markets it must consider whether or not those brand characteristics can be realistically used in those markets and, if not, where to make the necessary changes. Clearly, a well-established, or alternatively a simple, brand name would enable your firm to adopt a branding strategy that just utilized one brand name worldwide. The advantages to this approach are easy to spot: a high level of identification across markets along with the resulting increases in familiarity and the added bonus of a high degree of consistency and coordination in your firm's advertising and promotional efforts across multiple markets.

Unfortunately, many firms do not possess such a brand name, leading them to consider the proposition of modifying their brand—either partially or completely—for the firm's international markets. A partial brand name modification would be the use of Coke Light as an alternative to Diet Coke outside of the United States whereas a complete brand modification would be Walmart's use of the Asda brand in Great Britain. When these changes are made the goal is to ensure that the revised brand fulfills those requirements of a "good" brand name already discussed. No matter how much, or how little, your firm might choose to alter its brand name the goal is simple: to overcome the "foreignness" of your established brand in order to create a new, positive, product identity in your international market(s). A third alternative international brand strategy is to use your company as the primary brand rather than the different products your firm provides. Using this approach has the benefit of being flexible—there is no need for model/product-based promotions that increase the life span of your promotional efforts. Emphasizing your company name, rather than its products, also has the potential to facilitate communication across your various markets of operation. Companies who choose to use their company name as the anchor of their brand strategy often do this through the use of a corporate symbol or logo—a visual representation that overcomes language and other communication barriers.

Putting this all together, the keys to international brand success—in addition to the universal principles discussed at the outset—are these: translatable, transliterate, transparent, and transcultural. Just as the brand name needs to be easy to pronounce in any market, as you move into different international markets your brand must be translatable into other languages if the choice is made to either limit or completely avoid any brand name changes. Examples abound of brand translation mistakes, such as that of Coke's original brand attempt in China that used Chinese characters roughly translated as "bite the wax tadpole." Transliterate, on the other hand, deals with the need for the brand name to not only be translatable but also to convey the correct meaning. In the 1970s, Ford Motor Company placed a great deal of emphasis on its Pinto model as a potential global brand. The company found that, while it could be translated effectively into many different languages the meaning did not carry over—just one example is in Brazil where *pinto* is slang for small male genitals. Transparent means that consumers are able to see through the brand and get an undistracted perception of the product— the brand name cannot be confused with another product. Last, transcultural means the brand name effectively conveys the proper associations and expectations. Kinki Nippon Travel Agency—a Japanese firm—learned that the term *kinky* can produce associations that the firm was not intending (contrary to the impression the name gave in some markets, the firm did not provide sex vacations).

Before moving to product packaging, there is one other topic related to international branding strategy that must be noted: the problem of brand piracy. In the effort to ensure your product has an effective brand name it is easy to overlook the potential of having another firm steal your brand. Sometimes this comes in the form of imitation, which is a direct rip-off of your brand (i.e., placing your brand name on another product). A more subtle approach to brand piracy is "faking" where the brand, and often its logo, are presented in a way that is very close to the original but technically not in violation of the law in many markets. The use of an upside-down logo is a common form of brand faking. There is also the potential problem of brand preemption. This occurs when another individual or organization beats your firm to the registered legal use of your brand in another market. Irrespective of the form it takes, brand piracy is a serious problem as it directly affects the identity of your product in your international markets. Therefore it is incumbent upon your firm to not only ensure that all the criteria for a successful international brand are built into your brand strategy but also to ensure that your firm and its products will have a protected exclusive right to use that brand name.

International Packaging

This brings us then to packaging. In the U.S. market, packaging has often been viewed—at least when it comes to product strategy—as serving primarily a promotional function. In international markets the package has many product strategy–related functions and serves very much as a bridge between the product offering and its brand name. Four different constituencies must be taken into account in your firm's approach to international packaging strategy. The first is the customer. While the promotion function of packaging is still relevant in your international product management strategy, your international customer will also tend to place a great deal of emphasis on functional aspects of packaging—most specifically storage and features. Few consumers have the living space and capacity for storing and keeping products that U.S. consumers enjoy. This means that even in developed consumer markets, your customers will place a value on products that are easy to store. In England, the refrigerators in homes generally are significantly smaller than in America. This means, among other things, that the standard-sized milk container is a liter, not a gallon, with pint-sized containers being extremely popular as well. Further, your international customer will also expect the package to, wherever possible, enhance the product's usability. In the United States, we have come fairly late to this concept—squeeze bottles, pump containers, zip-sealed packages—but this has been the norm in markets around the world for decades.

There is also the issue of dealing with the other two important constituents: your firm's shippers and distributors in the host market. These pieces of the value chain are essential in bringing your product to market. But in order to maintain an effective value chain, your product's packaging must meet not only the customer's requirements but also those in the value chain. From the perspective of the shipper, the single most important aspect of the packaging of products relates to the ease of physical distribution—shipping. The shippers will give preference to products that are easy to transport—build up, break down, and that are not susceptible to damage. Anything your firm can do with its product packaging that will improve the ease of transportation will help to build relationships with your international shipper. Likewise, the distributors will also give preference to products whose packaging makes it easier for them to accomplish their responsibilities—particularly product merchandising and promotion. A package that is easy to stock and shelve, one that has a promotional appeal (i.e., easy to sell), and one that ensures a longer life span of the product (i.e., market relevancy) will, as is the case with the shipper, improve your firm's relationship with the distribution elements of your international value chain.

International Warranties and Service

The last product packaging constituent that must be attended to is the host government and it packaging requirements. Typically, a host government will have requirements for packaging that fall into one of three basic categories: special information, language, and promotional messages. Special information relates to the information about your product that the government will require be disclosed to the buying public and the form the presentation of that information takes. For example, the nutrition labels in the United States are standard and must disclose the nutritional content of several categories of potential ingredients and their contribution to an average daily diet—even if the product does not contain any of these ingredients. Similarly, in Europe there are also required nutritional labels, but they are different not only in the ingredients that must be disclosed but in the way these are measured (e.g., calories vs. kilocalories). Language requirements are the regulatory requirements that the packaging be presented in the host market language—not standardized in English. This type of requirement can vary widely depending upon the market your firm selects but can represent a significant packaging cost. The issue of promotional messages and the information they contain is related to what can be said in support of the product on the package. Claims that are common in the United States—such as "new and improved"—could easily need to be empirically documented before they can be used on a package in your firm's host market.

The last area of product management strategy to touch on is international warranties and service. The key issue with international warranties—the guarantee that the customer will receive a product that works and will continue to do so over a specified period of time—is the extent to which your firm standardizes its product's warranty. The most common mistake is to provide an extensive warranty to the product when the market does not expect that level of product support and the firm does not take into account the infrastructure and resources required to discharge a warranty in one, or more, international markets. The extent to which your firm provides a warranty for its product(s) should be determined by the market expectations, the product itself, and the ability to service (i.e., discharge the warranty) in markets other than your home market. Market expectations involve ascertaining exactly the degree to which your competitors warranty their products, the customer expectations regarding the product, and the overall service expectations of the market. The product characteristics—complexity, proclivity to breakdown, the extent to which a longer value chain might affect its marketability—would also influence the warranty placed on it. Finally, your firm's ability to service the product—that is, fulfill the warranty—must be thoroughly considered. Providing service in international markets can be very expensive, represents daunting logistical challenges, and is often overlooked—in terms of its complexity and expense—by U.S. firms. The bottom line when it comes to international product warranties and services is this: only provide what the host market expects and always keep a close eye on the cost-benefit of any warranty and service commitments to the product your firm makes.

SUMMARY

The heart of any successful international business model is a solid product strategy. This chapter addressed all facets of an international product strategy. Built around a discussion of the three cornerstones of a successful international product strategy—product concept determination, product design strategy, and product management—the chapter deals with the important issues of product standardization versus customization, the unique challenges associated with different levels of market development, product strategy and the market environment, the characteristics of an easily standardized product, branding, packaging, and warranties and service.

9

Making Your Product Viable: Creating an International Promotion Strategy

INTRODUCTION

In the previous chapter we discussed at length the issues involved in developing a successful product strategy for your firm's international markets. Understanding what unique values your product has to offer is a vital piece of your firm's international strategy. Without these unique bundle of values that your product represents there is no basis for international—indeed any—business model. Unfortunately, even companies with the most outstanding products do not have everything it takes for market success. There are countless examples of firms whose product orientation—directing resources almost exclusively toward producing the best product—resulted in market failure. The absence of a fully developed plan for communicating with the market about the product is a formula for disaster.

In this chapter we will touch on all the important facets of an effective international promotion strategy. These include creating an effective promotional message, choosing the right media to convey that message, determining the right mix of promotional tools, dealing with the problem of standardizing messages across markets, and ensuring your promotional strategy is consistent with—and supports—your firm's product strategy. Given that international operations frequently involve introducing your product to a market (i.e., making it a new product), being able to establish and implement an ongoing communication program in the form of a promotional strategy is essential in international business. Therefore, our discussion of promotional strategy will begin with the communication process.

PROMOTION IS COMMUNICATION

In any discussion of international promotion, and promotional strategy, it is tempting to immediately dive into the advantages and disadvantages of the various tools available to promote your firm's product as well as the different difficulties that can arise particularly in other markets. All of this, and more, will form the foundation of this chapter but before we can get into the specifics related to creating and implementing an international promotional strategy it is useful to remember what the bottom-line objective is in these efforts. Simply put, promotion is communication. Taking this notion one step further, international promotion is cross-cultural/cross-market communication—with all the potential pitfalls that go along with getting a message through in a different cultural environment.

To more fully understand why the communication process itself is so important let's consider the composition of the process, where your firm can control the process and where that control ends, the common problems that can be encountered, and how those problems can be effectively addressed. The communication process comprises three elements: the sender, the message, and the receiver. The sender (i.e., your firm) "encodes" its message (e.g., an advertising slogan or tagline) and then conveys that message to the target audience (i.e., the receiver). Upon receipt of this message, the receiver then "decodes," or interprets, the message. Simple enough. Where problems arise—especially in communication that involves senders and receivers from different cultures and markets and messages regarding products in which the receiver may have limited experience—is in the decoding part of the overall process.

The sending firm has control over the encoding process. It can choose how a message is constructed, what is communicated—and what it is not, and the means by which the message is disseminated in the market. However, once that message is sent out into the market, with very few exceptions, the sending firm relinquishes control of the process. This means in order to ensure that the communication objectives are met, the sending firm must be very careful in the course of encoding its message. The best way to avoid decoding difficulties is to consciously consider three types of what is called "selectivity" problems when creating a message.

Selectivity Problems

Like the communication process, the selectivity problems encountered in the decoding part of the process have three basic components. These are selective attention, selective distortion, and selective recall. The problem of selective attention recognizes that when a promotional message is communicated to its market audience there is no guarantee that those receivers will actually get the message. The nature of markets around the globe is such that all potential customers—whether they are individual consumers or business organizations—are constantly being bombarded with promotional messages. This volume of communications, combined with all the other distractions in the environment—known as "noise"—means that the first challenge in your promotional strategy is to induce the receiver to actually engage in the decoding process. In other words, the consumer must choose to pay attention to your firm's message rather than one of countless other distractions.

In international promotion this selective attention problem is frequently dealt with by the use of creativity when encoding the message and then presenting that message to the market. However, it is easy to misuse creativity in promotion—the most common problem being overcoming the issue of selective attention without actually accomplishing any communication goals. Instead, the firms that misuse creativity in their promotional message succeed in entertaining rather than communicating—a wasted effort. How to correctly approach the use of creativity in international promotions will be covered later in this chapter.

The second selectivity problem, which is only really a problem if selective attention is overcome, is selective distortion. This refers to the actual interpretation of the message and the fact that it is not uncommon for the receiver to misunderstand, or "distort," the message. This distortion can occur when the receiving audience either shows a tendency to "read into" the message (i.e., perceive an offer that is not intended) or "drops out" information (i.e., misses an important part of the message). The former can be a serious problem for your firm in an international market—a new market where your product is often viewed as "foreign." Whether intentional or not, this "reading into" a message—also known as "amplification"—can create substantial ill-will within the market. The problem of "drop out" may not be as serious in terms of creating negative feelings toward your firm and its product, but the end result is the same. When selective distortion occurs, the communication process is faulty. So what is the best way to deal with selective distortion? By accepting your firm's limitations within this new market—its lack of experience in operating in that market and the market's lack of experience with your firm and product—you are in a better position to create an effective message. The best way to deal with selective distortion in any message directed at an international audience is to keep the message as straightforward and direct as possible. Rather than assuming knowledge or experience on the part of the receivers, a better approach is to present as simple a message as possible, thus reducing the potential for misinterpretation.

Just because your message has been received and decoded does not mean that the communication objectives of your message have been accomplished. One piece is left—message recall. It is rare for your audience to receive a promotional message—even if they do correctly decode it—and be in a position to act on the message immediately. On the contrary, perhaps one of the biggest hurdles to overcome in promotion is to be able to ensure that the receiver can make a direct connection between the message and the product. Ask any consumer if she remembers an advertisement and chances are she can describe several, but has a hard time matching these messages with a specific firm or product. This is a recall problem.

Selective recall occurs most commonly when the receiver chooses—consciously or subconsciously—to remember those messages that are easiest to recall. Usually those are messages with which she is the most familiar. This can be a real problem for your firm when your message and product are new to a market. Some firms will attempt to overcome this difficulty through the use of creativity, but as we have already established this can result in simply entertaining the receivers. A better strategy with your international audience is to ensure there is a direct connection between the message and the product such as the use of prominent visuals in both promotion and packaging—an approach that succeeds in not only improving recall but can help overcome cultural and language barriers. The lesson setting the stage for effective international communication is this: the problems of selective attention, distortion, and recall can be most easily overcome through direct, uncomplicated messages that are tied as closely as possible to the reason for the message—the product.

THE INTERNATIONAL PROMOTIONAL MIX

The *promotional mix* is the term generally used to refer to the various means available to your firm for conveying your promotional message to the target audience. As is the case in your home market, the promotional mix options in international business come down to a choice between "push" approaches—communication mechanisms (e.g., personal selling) designed to push the message down the value chain—and "pull" approaches—communication mechanisms (e.g., advertising) designed to target the product's end-users and have them pull the product through the value chain using their demand for the product.

Personal Selling

Personal selling, which has the singular advantage of allowing your firm to adjust, adapt, and clarify its message during the decoding process, is an expensive and very involved means of sending a promotional message particularly in an international market. Because of this, personal selling tends most commonly to be the promotional tool of choice for companies involved in business-to-business markets. The ability to control the interpretation of the firm's promotional message is a huge benefit when crossing cultures and market environments. It can also help to facilitate the development of ongoing relationships between your firm and its customers. However, in order for personal selling to be an effective promotional tool there are some crucial points that must be taken into consideration that make international personal selling different from that in your home market.

One of the most obvious issues that arises is that of language barriers. The real advantage of personal selling over the other elements that compose the promotional mix is that it is interactive communication. This means that when crossing market boundaries it is almost guaranteed that one party in the communication process will be operating outside of his primary language—assuming that the firm does not employ a local sales force. It is true that U.S. companies do tend to have an advantage in when this situation arises given that English is the preferred language of business in the international market. However, it is important to remember the primary benefit of using personal selling, which is its ability to establish relationships. Having the cultural sensitivity to try and incorporate host-country language into the personal selling process can be very beneficial in creating the basis for a business relationship.

What your firm must avoid, however, is to automatically assume that using host-market language in the process requires that the local language is used exclusively. A common error that Americans, and American companies, make is in their estimation of what "fluent" means when it comes to another language. The truth is that Americans greatly overestimate their fluency in other languages; as a group we simply are not as proficient in other languages as we would like to think we are. If any firm has an inflated view of the language expertise of its employees it runs the risk of putting itself at a real disadvantage. Not only will it be more difficult to establish the relationships that are the foundation of personal selling, this scenario will put the firm at a disadvantage when it comes to understanding the nuance of any business discussions. It is highly advisable—especially when the other firm or target audience expects it—to use your home language (i.e., English) whenever possible. That is not to say that the host-market language should be avoided entirely—demonstrating cultural consideration through the use of a few carefully chosen words and phrases is in most cases preferable to insisting on using the host language and then proceeding to butcher the interaction.

Once the substantial barrier of language has been overcome in a personal selling strategy, there remains the related challenge of the actual interaction. No communication takes place in a vacuum and the international environment in which communication via personal selling takes place is heavily dominated by differences in business etiquette and negotiation patterns. This discussion could now spin off into a very detailed look into cross-cultural communication—which is beyond the scope of our topic. Suffice it to say, that as the environment in which these personal interactions becomes more dominated by cultural differences the logical solution would be to employ salespeople who are native to the host market.

The choice between using a home versus a host-country sales force is a complicated one. The main advantages of a home market sales force are primarily centered on ease of management. Home country employees are not only more easily controlled, there is no disconnect in the important area of compensation and motivation—your firm knows, or should know, exactly what these salespeople seek as rewards. Crossing cultures means that not only does it become more difficult to control your sales force, but there is the additional potential problem of what rewards they will seek out as motivation. Crossing cultures often means that employee management models are not transferrable. But using home market salespeople comes with other significant costs in the form of travel expenses, sales-related expenses, possibly even living allowance expenses, all of which can quickly add up. There is also the problem that home market salespeople may not be able to establish relationships in the market due to cultural differences. These suggest the use of host market salespeople, but remember the trade-off. Using this approach will require any firm to at least consider creating an employee management and compensation model that is uniquely suited to the host culture. High-quality market relationships may be a bonus of utilizing these local employees but the direct and indirect costs must be taken into consideration.

Advertising and Sales Promotions

The opposite end of the communication spectrum—advertising—involves mass, not personal, communication. Its primary strength is in its ability to convey your firm's message to a large number of targets. However, unlike personal selling, in its traditional forms it does not allow for message clarification or interaction with the target audience. Because of this, and the desire on the part of companies to have at least partial control over their promotional messages, international promotional strategies will utilize other elements of the promotional mix to either support, or in some cases, supplant the traditional primary promotional mix choices of personal selling versus advertising. Any of the alternative ingredients of your home market promotional mix could be employed but those most universally used internationally are sales promotions, sports marketing, and social media/marketing.

The objective of any sales promotion is to induce product trial. Sales promotion options range from coupons, rebates, and other "money-off" offers to trial samples of a given product. The desired result in all cases is to somehow motivate the targeted consumers to make a product purchase (i.e., try the product). The accepted rule for these sales promotions—in your domestic market—is to use them in support of your main promotional strategy, personal selling or advertising. The logic is straightforward: using sales promotions over an extended period of time can often result in the market expecting some form of deal from the firm and its products. A case in point is the U.S. automotive industry's overuse of rebates, which resulted in car buyers expecting additional monies off of their purchase on top of any negotiated purchase price.

This is certainly a disadvantage of sales promotions when used strictly as a means of inducing product trial/purchase, but in international markets there is another way of looking at some sales promotion techniques—that is, they can be employed to initiate a product-customer relationship. One of the greatest difficulties to overcome when your firm enters a new market is to motivate your target consumers to try its product. Reducing the risk to the consumer, whether perceived risk or financial risk, improves the chance that consumers will try the product and that is exactly the purpose of sales promotion. The difference is that our goal now is not to induce trial simply to achieve a sale but rather to engage in the sales promotion activities in such a way that the product trial is the first step in developing an ongoing relationship with the target consumers. The ability to provide a risk-free environment to "test" the product is ideal for initiating this type of customer relationship.

Whether or not a sales promotion program is successful in an international market is largely dependent upon the characteristics of the market in which it is used. It is important that the market view sales promotions as a culturally accepted approach to promotion. This means that they understand that an offer to try a product, one that may mean a greatly reduced or even eliminated cost to them as consumers, is not a reflection on the quality of the product. There is also the issue of the degree to which the consumers are familiar with not only the concept of sales promotions but also their expectations when it comes to similar competing products and the form those promotions take. It is true that overusing sales promotions can create "deal expectation" on the part of your consumer, but if this mistake has already been made by your competition it may be necessary at some level to meet the consumer's deal expectations. Finally, because sales promotions are designed to enable potential consumers to easily access a trial of the product, government and legal restrictions can impact how your firm implements its sales promotion program (e.g., in most markets worldwide, providing consumers with a sample taste of wine is directly tied to ongoing sales of a wine brand but many markets restrict or prohibit firms from providing consumers with free alcohol).

Sports Marketing

Sports marketing is also a very viable promotional tool in the international marketplace. Sales promotions can establish a tie between the customer and the product by inducing trial. Sports marketing can establish a close tie between the customer and the product. This is accomplished, not through actual experience with the product but by establishing an identification link using the product. Sports marketing enables consumers to see your firm and its products as a means of associating with a sporting event, team, or individual with which they would otherwise have no connection. With only a few exceptions, because of the nature and control of professional sports in the United States, sports marketing is not generally used as part of a promotional campaign—but it is widely used in other markets.

The real attraction of sports marketing is its ability to promote a firm, or a product, without the audience feeling that their attention has been intruded upon. By placing the message into the context of a sports environment— usually in the form of a logo—a large number of potential consumers are exposed to that message over an extended period of time without a sense that they are being "marketed" to. This can help to effectively overcome the problems of selective attention and recall (and to some degree selective distortion given the form the message is likely to take) as the message becomes part of the fabric of the sport, or sporting event. One of the unique abilities of this form of promotion is overcoming a negative country-of-origin effect. Associating a nondomestic firm or product with some aspect of sports that has no such baggage means that the local association with the sport attached itself to that nonlocal firm or product.

Sports marketing—which is really any association of your firm or its product with some facet of sports—can very easily serve as a culturally universal means of conveying your promotional message that, in addition, has the added bonus of wide coverage. Sports marketing is not limited by language, culture, or in many cases because of the wide broadcasting of sporting events, not even restricted by market/country boundaries. However, it does have one significant drawback. Sports marketing is very limited in its ability to convey anything but the simplest message. That means sports marketing can be effective in accomplishing an awareness communication objective, perhaps even an interest objective, but will be hard-pressed to achieve the higher level communication goals of desire and action.

Social Media

The other promotional tool that can be especially effective in international markets is social media marketing/promotion. In a sense, the use of social media can combine some of the best facets of personal selling, sales promotions, and sports marketing. It borrows a certain amount of personalization from personal selling in that social media is directed at individuals, using mechanisms like smart phones, which comes to them on an individual basis. The interactive benefits of sales promotions are also present, albeit not necessarily a direct interaction with the product but rather an interaction with the message. Twitter, social sites and applications such as Facebook or MySpace, and location applications like Foursquare and Gowalla, are highly interactive, which enables your firm to make its promotional message part of the interactive experience—and one that the target audience implicitly agrees to receive through engaging in these social media activities. Finally, the embedded benefits of sports marketing are present in social media as these types of messages do not require the receiver to stop an activity to engage the message—on the contrary the message becomes part of the social media experience. As is the case with sports marketing, any time your message can be layered into another experience the problem of selective attention can be overcome as can that of selective recall.

FORMULATING AN INTERNATIONAL PROMOTIONAL MIX STRATEGY

Creating a promotional strategy that is founded upon some element of the promotional mix other than the traditional means (i.e., personal selling versus advertising), such as sales promotions, sports marketing, and social media, is more common in international markets than it is for U.S. companies operating more or less exclusively in the U.S. market. The unique potential each of these alternatives has when it comes to overcoming the problems of cross-cultural/cross-market communications can be compelling depending upon the goals of your promotional strategy. However, in most cases, firms will still opt to use those promotional tools, and approaches to promotional strategy, with which they are the most familiar, which, in turn, means that advertising becomes a key element in promotional strategy.

Even taking into account the popularity of personal selling, at least with business-to-business organizations, advertising generally plays this prominent role in most firms' international promotional mix and the reasons are fairly straightforward. Advertising, while it can be expensive to create and place the ads, has a very favorable cost per contact. The base cost for advertising

can, on the surface, be intimidating but when the number of potential customers reached by the ad is taken into account advertising is an attractive
means of communication in an international market. Combined with this
low cost per contact is the mass reach associated with advertising. It is a very
attractive means of communicating given that advertising enables your firm
and its product to enter the market with maximum impact in a relatively
short period of time. There is also the issue of product control. Advertising
can be used as a mechanism to help control your product's price, positioning,
product use, and other aspects of your product strategy once it enters the
value chain. As we discussed in the chapter dealing with value chain strategy, a key area that must be attended to are the problems that can arise when
members of the value chain take charge of your product. Often this means
relinquishing control of many aspects of your product strategy. However, advertising can used to control the members of the value chain by creating
expectations in the market regarding your product that these members must
follow if the product is to be relevant. Generally, the various members of your
value chain will have little problem allowing a firm to control its product
strategy through advertising for the simple reason that they don't have to pay
for the advertising program.

So, considering the important benefits that are associated with advertising in international communications and promotion it is crucial to ensure that any ad campaign is done correctly the first time in order to avoid
negative results in the market. Although the cost per contact of advertisements is relatively low, the overall cost of an advertising program can be
expensive—and the costs for a good campaign are the same as the costs for
a bad campaign. No company wants to invest substantial sums in an ineffective initiative of any kind and that is exactly what can happen if your
firm is not careful in encoding its product message and selecting the media
through which the message will be communicated to the target audience.
As your firm could very likely have no direct, ongoing presence in a given
international market, its advertisements can also become your product's sole
representative in that market. The perceptions of the product, your firm,
and the overall "feel" of the ad will—in the absence of any other means of
interacting—create an identity among the ad's audience. Extending this idea
of advertisements as firm/product representative one step further, your ads
can then become a tangible component of your product provided the message can create a unique identity for your firm and/or your product. There
are countless examples of international firms operating in the United States
who have accomplished this very goal—Mercedes with its safety-oriented
commercials, Foster's Lager "It's Australian for Beer" campaign, and so forth.
The presence a well-developed ad campaign can create in an international
market—coupled with the ability to use the communications to control your

product and value chain strategies—make this a compelling choice around which to construct your firm's international promotional strategy.

STANDARDIZING YOUR MESSAGE: CHOICE CRITERIA

Just as your much of your product strategy efforts are centered on reconciling the advantages of a standardized product with the need to make adaptations for various markets, your firm's promotional strategy seeks—wherever possible and practical—to standardize its promotional strategy. The same advantages of standardization—economies of scale, consistency, and so forth— apply in both cases but like product strategy, if your promotional message is going to be relevant it may need to be altered. There are two areas that you and your firm must consider when addressing this issue of standardized promotional messages—choice criteria and transferability. Let's look first at choice criteria; that is, what would cause a consumer to choose to decode and act upon your market communication?

The Customer and the Message

In attempting to determine the likelihood that any potential customer will engage your promotional message enough to actually decode, and presumably act on, it a reasonable place to begin is with the complexity of the message. All else being equal, simpler messages are more likely to be decoded and recalled. However, depending upon the actual objective of the message, this complexity can vary. There are four basic communication objectives upon which virtually all promotional messages are based. These are attention, interest, desire, and action. Attention and interest are as stated— promotional messages with the goal of gaining attention and interest are simply trying to get the receiver to "turn his head." Desire and action are more involved—these present more complex messages as they are attempting to persuade the receiver to have a clear preference for the subject of the message (e.g., the product) and then make the ultimate move—the action of purchasing the product. The goals of attention and interest are typically considered to be the less complex and therefore messages with these objectives may be more readily standardized. Knowing the fundamental purpose of your promotional message is the important first step in making any determination regarding the extent to which the message might need to be adapted for your international market.

The next place to evaluate is the receiver—or your target audience. A target audience with higher levels of sophistication—education, income, living in an urban area, and so forth—is generally viewed as the type of audience that will be more acceptant of a standardized promotional message (i.e., one that is relatively easy to spot as being from a nondomestic source). The logic behind this rule of thumb is that these types of individuals have a wider experience of interacting with new concepts, ideas, and products by virtue of their presumed wider life experience. This can be especially advantageous for your firm as these are often the very individuals that are likely to compose your target market segment—that is, those willing and able to purchase a premium-priced imported product. Having made this general statement regarding the ease of standardizing your international promotional message, the fact remains that your firm and its product message must still be presented in such a way as to be relevant to your prospective customers, which means that even among relatively sophisticated consumers, message adaptations may still be required. This means we must go beyond labels such as "sophisticates" and look closer at the salient consumer behavior characteristics, as they relate to your firm's specific product, if we are to have a clear idea of the extent to which the promotional message must be adjusted in a new market.

Consumer Behavior and the Message

This deeper understanding of your target audience's consumer behavior relative to your firm's specific product offering can be viewed from two perspectives. On the one hand, there is the issue of the product itself and the actual "use" characteristics of the product as well as its important attitude attributes in this new market. On the other hand, there is also the issue of what drives the available media choices in terms of conveying your message to this target audience—things such as consumer and market preferences, characteristics of the market environment related to the sending and receiving of promotional messages, along with legal restrictions related to promotional messages.

Because the purpose of promotional strategy is to support your product strategy—and as we have seen the extent to which your product can be standardized in international markets is a predominant issue in your international product strategy—we must revisit some of the product characteristics and the related consumer behavior in attempting to ascertain how much, or how little, your promotional message can be standardized. These product characteristics that are key determinants in message standardization can be classified as relating to either purchase patterns, usage patterns, or the overall attitude toward the product.

As we have discussed previously, more often than not the acquisition of your product by consumers is not a singular event; that is, when consumers purchase a product they are not the sole individual influencing that purchase. Therefore, in order to ensure an effective message is communicated patterns related to who influences the purchase of a given product, who actually makes the purchase, and who uses the product must be taken into account when analyzing the possibility of standardizing some, or all, components of your promotional message. Depending upon the product, and its role in the consumption patterns in the international market, these purchase patterns can vary widely. Recent television ads, shown in the U.S. market, for Toyota SUVs show the primary spokesperson to be a boy extolling the virtues of the product—most notably the video system—from the backseat. Obviously, children don't purchase vehicles. But they do influence the purchase and use the product. Similarly, McDonald's ads in Japan focus on children interacting with SpongeBob Happy Meals—the food is secondary in the message. If a promotional message is going to succeed it must be constructed so that it reaches everyone involved with the product, not just the person or persons making the purchase itself.

The Product and the Message

In a similar vein, the message regarding your product must also be presented in a way that matches your international consumer's use of the product. Just as we discussed in the previous chapter, international product strategy must recognize that the value any given group of consumers can obtain from a product (i.e., the product uses) can change dramatically from one market to another. That can be a real advantage for your product—these alternative uses represent an expansion of your product offering with the resulting increase in market opportunities. In order to fully capitalize on these opportunities—and create a relevant promotional message—usage patterns (i.e., how the product is used, the circumstances under which it is used, the quantity consumed, etc.) in your message must be consistent with the role the product plays in that market. Breakfast cereal is shown in U.S. promotions as just that—a morning food. At the same time, in other markets a substantial proportion of these same products is consumed as snack food—a different usage pattern. Thus, visual portrayals of bowls of cereal and cartons of milk on the breakfast table give way to visuals depicting people of all ages eating the cereal directly from the box while watching television.

Lastly, in ensuring that your message matches the product characteristics of consumers in this host market, their overall attitude toward the product—all facets of the product—must be considered in this message standardization versus customization debate. This attitude, as it relates to promotional strategy, is focused on the advantages and disadvantages of your product—and whether or not these change as the product crosses consumer markets. Much of this centers on the actual product use, and any variations across markets, something already covered above. However, it also deals with indirect aspects of the product. For example, something as simple as a "Made in the USA" label can be either a real asset or a liability depending upon the market in which the product is placed. These differences in consumer preferences might suggest that, in an effort to standardize the message, such product characteristics be deemphasized—but doing so might mean an important competitive advantage of your product offering (at least in some markets) is absent from the message.

An additional element in this evaluation of choice criteria is media availability. In our earlier discussion of the promotional mix we touched on the fact that not all means of conveying a message might be options for your firm and its promotional strategy. Some of this has do to with the legal restrictions that exist in markets around the world. Over the years, Playtex has encountered numerous challenges in the way in which it can show its bras in advertisements—some markets allow the product to be shown, but without the female form. Other markets prohibit the use of anything female, period. Still others allow the use of women in the advertisements, but not underwear. A real challenge and one that requires significant adaptation of the presentation of the promotional message for a relatively universal product.

The other areas of media, and the availability of media, that impact message standardization in the choice criteria evaluation have to do with consumer preferences and the characteristics of the environment in which the promotional activities take place. Whether we realize it or not, consumers in a market frequently have preconceived notions of where they expect to be presented with different promotional messages. In the United States we do not expect to see messages for financial investment services during episodes of *Scooby Doo*—nor do we expect Happy Meal ads on the Military Channel. For maximum effectiveness, the message must be presented to the target audience in the time, place, and format in which it is most receptive—such as in the French market where coupons for food products are replaced by in-store samples and demonstrations. This is a promotional mix challenge that has a direct impact on the evaluation of message choice criteria. There is also the potential problem of ensuring the environment characteristics of the media employed to convey the message are consistent across markets. In the U.S. market billboards have traditionally had the advantage of a long market life—but these same billboards in Middle Eastern markets have a greatly reduced life span due to the heat, wind, and sand to which they are exposed. Putting all these issues together reveals that the first and most important issue to address when making any determination regarding the possible standardization of your message across markets is making the message relevant in your chosen market(s).

STANDARDIZING YOUR MESSAGE: TRANSFERABILITY

The evaluation of choice criteria has much to do with your ability to move an existing message—its content and the means by which it is communicated—across markets, consumers, and their individual cultures. There is still, however, an aspect of promotional strategy and communication that also needs attention—the presentation of the message. If choice criteria is about the content of the message and the degree to which it can be standardized, transferability is about how the message is crafted—its tone (e.g., informative vs. humorous), sensory appeals (e.g., visuals, language, colors), and message source (e.g., endorsers and spokespeople). This "crafting" of a message is also known as creative presentation. The use of creativity in a promotional message can be a very effective means of reducing the various selectivity problems we have discussed. Creativity is a powerful communication tool, but it is also one that is easily misused and can be problematic when it comes to crossing cultures. It is a common error to mistake entertainment for communication, but it is a crucial error to avoid. The objective of your promotional activities is most certainly not to entertain the target audience—it is to communicate a clearly defined message to that audience.

Creativity in International Promotion

The purpose of creativity is to enhance the message through a reduction in selective attention, distortion, and recall and also, by extension, to enhance the product in a controlled setting. In looking at what might prevent the effective use of creativity in an international promotional message there are five categories of barriers. Some involve culture and communication issues, some outside influencers, and still others deal with the characteristics of the communication environment in the given market. Each individually has the capacity to substantially impact all areas of creativity—any combination of substantial barriers in more than one of these areas may mean a complete overhaul of your firm's creative approach to promotional strategy and the accompanying messages.

Culture can affect your firm's ability to use certain types of creative approaches directly through cultural barriers and less directly through communication barriers. However, the recurring theme in this assessment of how much, or how little, creativity can be used (and in what form) is the same: how much your overall promotional strategy, and the means by which the message is presented, must be changed for a specific market. The actual cultural barriers, related to creativity in promotions, that can represent the biggest problem are those related to the credibility of the message source.

Oftentimes, creativity is used in the presentation of the promotional message not just to gain attention but also to increase the credibility of the message by transmitting the message in such a way that the receivers can more readily identify with the message. People can be used to accomplish this aim, but it is vitally important that any use of individuals as spokespersons for your firm and its products be consistent with the culture in which the message is being communicated. Other cultures can be more sensitive to gender differences when it comes to receiving promotional messages and the perceived credibility of those messages. Similarly, what might be an important celebrity endorser in one market may be unknown in another market—for example, Wayne Rooney (a very prominent English soccer player) was recently dropped as a celebrity endorser by Coca Cola largely due to his lack of recognition outside of England. These sorts of examples are numerous, but the lesson is the same: the use of creativity to raise the credibility of the message can be bound by cultural differences that can exist across markets.

Barriers to Communication

Communication barriers operate in a similar fashion. These barriers have more to do with the underlying means by which creativity is used to communicate a specific message. One of the most common communication barriers is the "tone" a promotional message adopts. Humor, something that is used widely in U.S. promotional messages for all sorts of goods and services, is an excellent example of a communication barrier. It can be very difficult to be successfully humorous in another culture and another language. Using a humorous tone in your message—and failing—will, at best, result in your product and its message being viewed as "silly" and, at worst, can offend the market. The most acceptable approach in trying to overcome cultural and communication barriers when employing creativity in your promotional strategy is to keep it as simple as possible and always remember the end goal of your promotional activities is to communicate not to entertain.

The next category of barriers to using creativity—and standardized creativity especially—are those that are present in the external marketplace; specifically, legislative and competitive barriers. As was the case with obligatory and discretionary strategy adaptations, changes in the creative presentation of your promotional message may be required for the message to go out or required in order to ensure the maximum effectiveness of your message. In analyzing the transferability of your creative strategy, the legislative barriers are similar to those already discussed above in the area of choice criteria. How these impact the use of creativity is generally in one of two areas: the type of message allowed (e.g., the information conveyed and the claims/statements that are made) and in the media allowed (e.g., in a market where televisions advertisements are strictly controlled the potential for a visual creative strategy may be severely limited). There is little that can be done to manage these legislative barriers and, unlike the other barriers to creativity, it is mandatory to adhere to any legislative dictates.

The competitive barriers, on the other hand, do not demand compliance— but failure to recognize these as potential limiting factors in your message presentation will result in a reduction in the efficacy of the promotional message. The single most problematic competitive barrier is often described as *ad expectation*. This term refers to the fact that, as has been touched on earlier in our discussion of choice criteria, the competition can create expectations within the market regarding the type of message, its tone, timing of delivery, and media in which the message is presented. This all adds up to your firm needing to conform to these expectations if the target audience is going to be in an ideal mindset to receive your product message. For years in the United States, Heineken beer wrestled with the problem of having a premium-priced imported beer in a market where the product was not promoted in a serious way—resulting in a rapid loss of market share when more and more competing imported beers hit the market with messages that were more in keeping with the audience's expectations, à la Corona's relaxed, tropical promotions.

The final barriers to your firm's ability to transfer the creative component of its promotional strategy are the implementation barriers. These have to do with the "mechanical" aspects of the media used to transmit a message. We do not always give these much thought simply because in the U.S. market they are not an issue. Problems such as printing technology, production facilities, Internet connectivity, high-definition media and broadband, and the availability of mass media (e.g., television, radio, and unlimited web access) are no barriers to U.S. firms in their home market. The U.S. market has always had the widest possible range of creative tools available—often resulting in their overuse, leading to messages that entertain, but do not communicate. This is not necessarily the case in your host markets. It is very common in international markets for the most significant barrier to creative strategy to be these implementation barriers. Having a clear picture of the presence of any implementation barriers is absolutely essential prior to the actual creation of your firm's message, and the problems associated with failing to take these into account should not be underestimated.

COORDINATION OF PRODUCT
AND PROMOTIONAL STRATEGY

In our discussion, both in this chapter and the previous one, we have dealt with the question of standardization—product and promotion. We must remember that each of these areas must be consistent with and support the other. A promotional strategy is useless unless it has substance to communicate (i.e., a product to "talk" about); similarly the product strategy is useless unless there is a deep understanding of what the product is and what it represents to your international customers (i.e., its "values"). The final step in strategy formulation is to bring the product and promotional strategy together. This strategy coordination leaves your firm with four possible options: same product/same message, same product/different message, product adaptation/same message, and product adaptation/message adaptation.

When your firm concludes that the value appeal for its product is essentially unchanged from one market to the next a virtually unaltered promotional message is probably appropriate. Cross Pens, pens that are made of nonprecious, nondisposable metal such as chrome, target young professionals around the world with the same product and the same basic message: "Cross Pens: The Impression Goes beyond Words." Peanut M&Ms are also unchanged from a product perspective in most markets around the world, but because the value of the product changes (e.g., some markets view peanut M&Ms as health food, not candy) the message appeal and target audience are different. Toothpaste is an example of a product where product adaptation is required, but the message is unchanged—the reason to purchase and use toothpaste is basic: clean breath and teeth. U.S. producers of toothpaste, however, have found that in some markets the consumers don't find the "clean breath and teeth" message credible coming from a product that looks like blue gel and tastes like bubblegum. Hence, the message remains the same, but the toothpaste is made more "medicinal" (i.e., white paste with a mint flavor). Product adaptations/message adaptations can often be the most challenging and the hardest to maintain over time. A regional U.S. toilet paper manufacturer attempted to enter a European market using toilet paper with English lessons printed on the roll. The product had a value appeal that went beyond just the toilet paper "performance" with a supporting promotional message. This adapted approach worked, but only for a short period of time. The novelty was not sustainable and the product was viewed, after about 18 months, as a fad—and quickly faded from the market. This approach can be very difficult to sustain over time if the life span of the unique product and promotional strategies are not seriously considered.

SUMMARY

Effective promotion is all about effective communication. In international operations the ability to successfully communicate to your chosen target market(s) is complicated by a number of factors including different perceptions of your firm and its product, different consumer behavior patterns, different communication tools, and the need to adjust the basic message as cultures are crossed. This chapter discussed at length the various issues that must be addressed, and problems that must be overcome, in order for a firm to be in a position to create a successful promotion strategy. Because no firm can achieve market success simply on the merits of its product—no matter how superior—some fundamental, important points regarding international promotion should be noted. Whenever cultures and languages are mixed the power of visual communication should never be overlooked. Any firm with a product that can be visually portrayed should leverage the ability of visual language in an effort to minimize these culture and language differences. In addition, the media that compose the international promotional mix can be very difficult to evaluate and the rules and regulations that govern each promotional tool can mean that a firm must be prepared to employ new and different mechanisms for communicating. Finally, as soon as cultures are crossed the potential for misunderstanding is substantial. At the very least this misunderstanding means a failure in the communication process; at the most it can mean that the message offends or alienates some or all of the host market. This means that any promotional activities should focus a great deal of attention on managing the message encoding process.

10

Putting It All Together: Creating an International Business Plan

INTRODUCTION

In this chapter we will bring together all of the different topic areas discussed through the previous chapters in order to create a road map for developing and implementing an international business plan designed specifically for your firm. We will begin by reviewing the key imperatives associated with international business strategy and then move on to strategic planning, assessment of the different aspects of the international environment, checklists and scorecards that will assist you and your firm in determining its level of readiness as well as identifying areas that must be addressed in order to maximize the likelihood of success in your international operations. The chapter will conclude with a section directed at different outside resources dedicated to assisting U.S. firms in their international endeavors.

Before even thinking about the logistics of putting together a plan for international operations it is very important to strategically ideate the reasons why you think you will be successful at exporting. The following is meant to serve as "thought" areas to get you started in the right direction.

Why International Operations?

There are a number of imperatives in the current and evolving marketplace that would cause firms of virtually any size to consider international operations. However, the most compelling reasons are the need for growth, the opportunity to increase market share in the global market, and the ability to gain competitive advantage.

- Growth—growth opportunities at home are becoming limited
- Market Share—your firm can provide skills or core competencies in markets where these are lacking or underdeveloped
- Competitive Advantage—your firm can preempt competitors in that market(s)

Each of these imperatives can be viewed independently or in some combination; however, their importance to any given firm might shift as the priorities of the firm changes.

The Strategic Process

One area that we did not explicitly touch on is the strategic process. Many firms have this institutionalized already, and the actual process itself does not significantly vary when a firm moves from domestic to nondomestic operations. At the same time, it is important for your firm to understand the importance of the process and how the issues related to international operations fit into the strategic process. We will integrate this into our discussion in the next section, but here are the key highlights in the process as they relate to the strategy of international business.

- Companies considering international operations need to make these activities an integral component of their strategic plan, not a separate activity
- Strategic plans consist of objectives (goals), strategies, and tactics
- Many companies confuse strategies and tactics for objectives
- A common practice for most companies is to create either a three- or five-year strategic plan on an annual basis. However, this may be too long, or too short, a period. Strategic plans must have a level of flexibility as they may need to change differentially over the defined time period

Defining Value: What Is Value?

Oftentimes firms view value only in the context of price and cost. Consumers across the globe, however, tend to view value from the viewpoint of maximizing values—of all types—and minimizing costs. The important thing to remember, especially in the context of international strategy, is that in the eyes of your global customer value is more than product quality and costs extend beyond the financial. Value can be product value (functionality and features) but it also extends to service value (ensuring product value over time), personnel value (the customer's comfort level when interacting with firm employees), and image value (e.g., the value of your brand). On the other hand, costs can be financial, but there are also time costs (the lag between purchase decision and product receipt), energy costs (the effort required to access the product), and image costs (the psychological costs associated with a product somehow perceived to be inferior). This means you and your firm should carefully weigh the question, what is value?

- From the company, or firm, perspective value was traditionally price–cost
- It was traditionally approached using one of two strategies: Low Cost = Lowest Production Costs or Differentiation = Product Attractiveness
- The best approach is the most profitable blending of the two approaches, resulting in superior value (see the different values and costs above)
- Value from the international consumer perspective involves:
  - Is it financial cost–benefit only?
  - What defines your product quality?
  - What about the relevant intangibles or various values and costs?
  - What about differentiation and aspiration?
  - What about brand loyalty?
  - What about customer service?

Having a larger view of all the relevant values and costs gives your firm more means of gaining competitive advantage and achieving success in non-domestic markets.

Strategic Positioning

Strategic positioning is about both your firm and your product(s). A firm should have a clearly defined plan as to how it will present itself and the role it will play in its host market. Much of this is dealt with in the market entry strategy. The firm must also have a clear idea as to the identity, or positioning, of its product in this new market, or markets.

- How does your company plan to enter and operate within the international marketplace?
- What specific values can be leveraged?
- What specific consumer costs can be reduced?

In practice your firm and product positioning should be based on the most efficient and credible response to your target audience in each market in which your firm chooses to operate.

Rationale for Global Expansion

While there are a number of reasons that would cause a firm to engage in international operations, from a strategic perspective your firm must understand its own specific rationale for moving outside of the domestic business environment.

- Location Advantages—realize location economies
- Cost Advantages—realize greater cost economies
- Expertise Advantages—leverage core competencies
- Skill Advantages—leverage and transfer skills

Any one of these represents a sound basis for international operations. Obviously, not all firms have distinct competencies in all of these areas but it may be that having a clear superiority in just one can form the basis for competitive advantage in another market.

Location Economies

The market(s) in which your firm selects to operate can provide economies that translate into competitive advantage in both your host and home markets. However, it is essential that not only the potential benefits but also the possible problem areas be taken into account.

- Cost advantages from performing business operations at its most optimal location
- Global network where each activity in the value chain is optimally located so that value, for all parties, is maximized and costs are minimized
- Be cognizant of potential location-related problems (e.g., transportation costs/trade barriers, political and economic risks)

As many U.S. companies have discovered, expanding operations into other countries can result in more revenue opportunities in these new host markets, but these expanded operations can also lead to increased efficiencies—and higher revenues—in their home market as well.

Cost Economies via Experience Effects

Another area that impacts international strategy, and can lead to increased revenue, involves the role of knowledge and experience. Being able to leverage knowledge and experience can create efficiencies that result in cost economies and ultimately higher profits.

Remember:

- Moving up the experience curve can produce production cost reductions occurring over the life of the product
- Leveraging learning effects means gaining the necessary experience to operate more efficiently and effectively
- Knowledge can create economies of scale—more is better

There are two types of knowledge identified with international business: objective and experiential. Objective knowledge can be obtained from secondary sources—like this book. Experiential knowledge is gained through actual international experience. Both are necessary for success in international business.

The Importance of Local Responsiveness: Things to Keep in Mind

When your firm engages in international operations the relevant differences that might exist—and their potential for affecting your plans—should always be at the forefront of the decision-making process. The differences most likely to influence your international activities are:

- Differences in local consumer tastes and preferences
- Differences in local infrastructure and practices
- Differences in local distribution channels
- Differences in host government requirements and regulations
- Necessary changes in product offerings and marketing strategies to specific national conditions in a host market
- The problems in creating and operating a comprehensive value chain in each major nondomestic market

OBJECTIVES, STRATEGIES, AND TACTICS: MAKING THE DISTINCTION

Is it an objective, a strategy, or a tactic? Even the most experienced international business decision maker can have difficulties making the correct distinction. Because we have been taught to be action-oriented in business, we can quickly mistake tactical statements for objectives or strategies. In most cases, however, these are the action items needed to support the strategies in order to achieve the objectives.

In an effective, actionable, international business plan, the highest level of analysis is the objectives. These are the stated, quantifiable, and measurable results that you desire or plan to achieve. An objective is then further defined by a strategy or set of strategies. These are broad descriptive statements on how you intend on achieving the objectives. Finally, each strategy is then supported by one or a number of tactics. These are the detailed action-based processes or programs that you will follow in order to successfully meet the strategy and achieve the objectives. Let's look at each of these in more detail.

Objectives

A strategic objective defines *what* needs to be accomplished. It must be specific. The objective must focus on a single goal. It must also be measurable. The results must be quantifiable. The objective must also relate to a specific time period. Finally, it must focus on affecting behavior (e.g., retaining current customers, growing new customers, purchasing products, cross-selling products).

Examples of objectives include:

- Retain 70% of existing customers in 2012
- Increase the average number of products held by existing customers from 1.2 to 2.0 products during the next 12 months
- Increase customer satisfaction by 7% over the next two quarters
- Increase nondomestic business by 20% in 2012

In creating and writing straightforward, actionable objectives you need to remember the following rules.

All objectives must:

- Be specific in focus
- Be measurable
- Defined within a specific time period
- Relate to a specific target market(s)
- Focus on affecting some behavior or performance

Objectives should be kept to one sentence and their rationale to one brief paragraph. Your firm should invest considerable time in developing these objectives; remember they are the focus of your entire plan. Don't necessarily feel limited to one objective. It is quite possible that your firm may need multiple objectives with each focusing on a narrower target market or specific area of behavior. Finally, don't mistake slogans for objectives. Statements such as "to provide world class service" or "be the best" are slogans. They are not quantifiable, time-specific, or behavior-defining and do not reflect results that can be measured.

Strategies

Strategies describe *how* the objectives will be accomplished and provide the overall direction the detailed tactics will follow. A strategy is a broad directional statement indicating how the objective will be achieved. It identifies the method for accomplishing the objective by providing the direction for the more specific, action-oriented tactical plans and tools.

Where objectives are specific, quantifiable and measurable, strategies are descriptive. After reading the strategies, management should have a good overall understanding of how your firm plans to achieve the objectives. The actual details of these strategies will be spelled out in the subsequent tactical tools and processes.

Examples of strategy statements include:

- Develop a unified host country marketing program focusing on one common promotional campaign
- Promote heavily during major seasonal periods
- Increase advertising spending as a percent of sales to be competitive with the host country market leader
- Develop new products, or modify existing products, in order to attract adults 55 years or older
- Concentrate on gaining incremental business in Europe
- Develop image advertising to build long-term sales and brand loyalty
- Develop an ongoing research tracking study to monitor consumer awareness, attitudes, and behavior

In creating and writing focused strategies you and your firm need to remember some basic rules. First, make strategies descriptive statements of how you will achieve your objectives. Second, don't let these strategies become too execution-oriented. Instead, keep your strategies broad and directional. Third, and finally, don't write long, elaborate strategies. Your strategic statements should be simple and focus on a single idea.

Tactics

Tactics are the specific short-term activities, processes, or initiatives that must be accomplished in order to achieve the objective. Tactics are derived from these related strategies and are those detailed action items or initiatives that must be successfully completed in order to meet the objectives.

Examples of tactical statements include:

- Promote exporting through a direct mail campaign during the second and fourth quarters of 2012

- Increase brand awareness by targeting brand spots to high market areas during the first and third quarters of 2012
- Test wireless project during the third quarter of 2012
- Attend three to five international trade fairs during March–June 2012

As was the case with strategic statements, in creating and writing tactics there are certain rules that must be followed. Remember, a tactical statement should be very specific and related to only one initiative or project. Tactical statements should be action-oriented (i.e., what will be done, to whom, by when). Tactical statements should be short, concise, and provide management with at least a basic understanding of what the initiative will be. Tactical statements should be supported by the actual tactical plan. That is, what steps will need to be accomplished, what resources will be needed, during what time frame?

Steps in Developing an International Business Plan

By using the guidelines above, and incorporating the issues discussed in the first section dealing with the strategy of international business, developing your international business plan can be performed in a reasonably straightforward manner by adhering to the following steps:

Step 1   Define Corporate Mission →
Step 2   Develop Business Plan →
Step 3   Complete a Four-Step Environmental Assessment →
- Situation Analysis—Basis View
- Product Positioning Analysis
- Portfolio Analysis
- Problem and Opportunity Analysis
Step 4   Develop Marketing Objectives →
Step 5   Select Marketing Strategies →
Step 6   Develop Tactical Plans →
Step 7   Create Budget/Pro Forma Financial Statements →
Step 8   Develop Implementation Strategy →
Step 9   Develop Control and Monitoring Systems →
Step 10 Update Plan

It is very important to remember that strategic planning and implementation is an ongoing feedback system. Each time you update the plan, you will need to go back to Step 1 and make any revisions or changes as needed throughout the entire process. Strategic plans are made up of objectives, strategies, and tactics. Objectives are the *quantifiable, measurable results* you want to achieve. Strategies are *broad descriptive statements* that define how you plan to achieve the results. Tactics, then, are the *actual tools and processes* that you will implement to successfully accomplish the strategy and, therefore, meet your objective.

ASSESSING THE ENVIRONMENT

In this section we will synthesize the key areas of Chapters 2–4 into a concise toolkit for assessing the international business environment and the markets in which your firm is contemplating operations.

Demographic Assessment

Understanding a country means understanding its population. Knowing the country's population structure allows one to understand current, and predict future, behavior. Demographics are directly related to other factors such as economics, culture, religion, education, and technology. In many cases, a country's age and gender breakdown is extremely important for the country's business and overall future attractiveness as a market.

A demographic assessment tells your firm how large and diverse your potential audience or target market is. It also provides your firm with general information or parameters before you actually enter a given market. Finally, it identifies possible barriers to reaching target market segments and allows your firm to anticipate the future.

At the same time, the demography of a market is extremely important to understanding the impact of the physical environment of the country, or countries, in which your firm is considering international operations. A country's physical environment consists of such things as geographical location, size, territorial boundaries, transportation infrastructure, natural resources, and climate. Remember that the physical environment directly impacts transportation and commercial flows, politics, economics, and cultural differences even within a country. Much of these data are available on various country websites or from secondary sources such as the CIA's *World Factbook* or Michigan State University's Global Edge website.

Key questions to ask when conducting a demographic assessment include the following:

Understanding the Population

- How large is the current population?
- Is the population growing, stable, or in decline?
- What about immigration (in) and emigration (out)?

- How is the population dispersed?
- Is the population predominantly urban or rural?

Understanding the Age Composition

- What is the current age breakdown of the population?
- Is the population becoming younger or older?
- What influence does the older population have on the society?
- What influence does the younger population have on the society now and will have in the future?
- How does the age of the population relate to other socioenvironmental factors?
- What about birth and mortality rates?

Understanding Gender Composition

- What is the ratio of females to males in the country?
- What percentage of women are of childbearing age?
- Are societal roles strictly defined by gender?
- What factors (positively or negatively) affect childbearing in the country?

Understanding the Physical Environment

- Where are the major population centers located?
- How accessible are the population centers by air, water, rail, and highway?
- Are there natural boundaries that may impact the movement of your product into the country and then distribution throughout the country?
- What is the climate like and what effect, in any, will that have on your product?

Economic Assessment

An economic assessment is essential in order to identify whether or not the market your firm is planning to enter can sustain you and your product. Research has shown that the economic condition of a country receives the greatest amount of attention from companies thinking about international operations.

A key factor in this assessment is the actual purchasing decision process, including how much of a product people buy, why it is purchased and used, and which products they choose to buy. These are all largely influenced by economic factors. It may well be that only small groups of consumers within the country have the wherewithal to purchase your product. Is this group sufficiently large enough to offset the costs of providing your product to them? At the same time, is the country moving to a more advanced stage of economic transition where purchasing power is expected to dramatically increase in the near future? If so, which is more important to you: an immediate short-term return with limited outcomes or a slightly longer approach with a greater profitability potential? These are strategic questions that need to be answered if your firm plans to be successful in the target country.

An economic assessment involves five categories of questions:

Understanding the Country's Level of Development

- How economically developed is the country?
- Is it an undeveloped nation (third world)?
- Is it primarily an agrarian economy?
- Is it a developing nation (second world)?
- Is it primarily a manufacturing economy?
- Is it a developed nation (first world)?
- Is it primarily a service economy?

Understanding the Country's Demographic Transition Status

- If the country is underdeveloped, is it showing rapid population growth?
- If the country is a developing nation, is it showing slower population growth?
- If the country is a developed nation, is there little natural growth, with most, if any, increases coming from immigration?

Understanding the Country's Economic System

- Is the economic system predominantly an open system (e.g., free market)?
- If an open system, what are the rules/regulations governing it?
- Is the economic system predominantly a closed system (e.g., government-controlled)?
- If a closed system, is there any room for entrepreneurship?

- How much (if any) flexibility is there to operate within the stated economic system?
- Does the government view its primary role as a facilitator or provider?
- How does the government deal with the concept of "fair" competition?

Understanding the Country's Attractiveness as a Revenue-Generating Market

- What are the country's primary sources of economic development?
- What metrics (e.g., gross domestic product) are used to assess the strength of the economic system?
- What is the quality and quantity of demand for products and services?
- What is the country's availability of raw and component materials?
- What is the country's availability of labor and capital?

Understanding Consumer Purchasing Power

- What does consumer income distribution look like for the country?
- How would quality of life be assessed in the country?
- Where are the consumers with the greatest purchasing power located?
- Is purchasing power limited or is it expected to grow across the different classes of consumers?

Competitive Assessment

In the course of conducting assessments of the various components of the international environment, your firm would be remiss if the competitive environment was ignored. Too frequently firms make assumptions regarding what firms and products represent their primary competitive threat. Because the value the customer in another market seeks may be very different from that associated with your home market, it is always worthwhile to consider your firm's position relative to gaining competitive advantage in any given market. Assessing competitive advantage revolves around these basic questions:

- Who are your competitors currently? Are these likely to change in the future? Why?
- How important to the competition is a specific market?
- What are the competition's unique strengths?
- What are the competition's exploitable weaknesses?
- What are the likely future changes in your competitor's strategy(s)? Will these have a significant impact on the market?

Technological Assessment

Doing a technological assessment allows your firm to look at the country as a prospective marketplace that may, or may not, be ready for your products(s). Keep in mind that while your product may not require technology, its supply chain, marketing, sales, distribution, and servicing might.

Just some of the questions that need to be addressed include, what is the target country's level of sophistication with computer technology? Is it readily available and used by businesses and the residents? How available is what you might consider common everyday technology such as personal computers, mobile telephones, and the Internet?

The transfer of technology is also a critical factor in economic development. Technology transfer has become extremely important between, and within, countries due to advances in global communication and the economic interdependence of countries. The transfer of technology has allowed less developed countries to compete on a regional and global basis and, more important, has enabled them to integrate innovative products into their environment at unprecedented rates.

As discussed in Chapter 2, the questions to ask fall into four categories:

Understanding the Level of Technological Education

- What is the educational level of the population?
- Is advanced technology taught at all levels in the school system?
- Is equipment available/accessible for students to use?
- Are there special schools that teach the latest technology?
- What is the country's attitude about technology?

Understanding the Level of Technological Advancement

- What is the country's level of technological advancement?
- Is technology relatively new?
- Is it highly controlled? Who controls it?
- Is it accessible to the masses?
- How expensive is it?

Understanding the Technological Infrastructure

- What is the technology infrastructure like?
- Is there a plentiful and continuous supply of electricity?
- Are there a sufficient number of towers and other hardware for such things as cell phones?

- How hard and expensive is it for companies to replace and/or update equipment?
- Does the country have a plan or vision for technology in the future?

Understanding the Level of Technology Transfer

- Is the technology easily transferable?
- Do the systems speak to each other within the country?
- Do the systems speak to other systems outside the country?
- How hard is it to transfer comparable equipment and software in and out of the country?
- Are there legal sanctions and rules?
- Are there differences in equipment standards and protocols?

Assessing the Legal Environment

In international operations firms need to be able to recognize the legal significance of their business-related and marketing activities in each of the countries in which they do business. Your firm needs to be aware that the legal environment is a complex network of laws and regulations that exist on at least three levels. First are the laws of your own country. Second are the laws of the country or countries to which you are considering exporting. Third are any international laws that might affect your transactions at any number of levels.

Legal systems vary from country to country. Your firm is very likely to discover that rules that might make sense in your home market may be very different in other host markets. Keep in mind, however, that in order to operate successfully in those markets, your firm must understand the various laws and regulations both at the "letter" and "spirit" levels. These laws and regulations may not be concerned only with product entry into the market, they may also be concerned with product ownership, distribution, advertising, and packaging.

Buyers and sellers are also subject to international law, which may be defined as that body of rules that regulates relationships between countries or other international legal persons. The principal sources of international law are treaties and conventions. These are created when several countries reach agreement on a certain matter and bind themselves to it by authorizing their representatives to sign a document embodying that agreement. Essentially, they have entered into a contract that obliges them to do something or to refrain from doing something. Failure to comply is the equivalent of breach of contract.

Before a country can comply with the provisions of a treaty or a convention, it must have signed the original protocol (i.e., the original treaty document or minutes of the convention). Once a country has signed the protocol, the method of enforcement depends on the terms of the treaty or convention. A common way of taking action against a country is by imposing sanctions against it. Sanctions may take many different forms and can be applied with varying degrees of severity.

Questions pertaining to the legal environment in a country include:

- What trade barriers exist?
- What trade treaties/agreements does the country have with the United States?
- Is the country a member of a regional trade association (e.g., EU, NAFTA, ASIAN)? What are tariffs/taxes levied at products imported from other countries in general and in your industry in particular?
- Does the country have any quotas related to your firm's products/services that you wish to export?
- Are there any special licensing or other fees?

Assessing the Political Environment

No matter how attractive the prospects of a particular country or region are, doing business there might prove to be financially disastrous if the political structure of the host government is not understood. The political environment in which the firm operates (or plans to operate) will have a significant impact on a company's international activities. The greater your firm's level of involvement in foreign markets, the greater the need to monitor the political climate of the countries in which business is conducted. Changes in government often result in changes in policy and attitudes toward nondomestic firms. It is important to keep in mind that a nondomestic firm operates in a host country at the discretion of that government. The government controls the environment and can either encourage international business activities by providing opportunities for trade and minimizing the barriers to entry and ongoing business, or discourage these activities by imposing entry restrictions and maintaining strict regulatory and oversight systems. Many governments change over time and your firm must be continuously aware of changes in government and governmental attitudes.

Today, nearly all governments play active roles in their countries' economies. Of primary concern is the stability of the target country's political environment. Instability could lead to a company having to reduce its operations in the market or to withdraw from the market altogether. This is extremely problematic when there are frequent changes of the groups or regimes in power. Keep in mind that the new government may not have been privy to the original agreements with the most recent government and may have totally different attitudes and policies toward international business. These changes can impact significantly on both the exporter's current and longer-term ability to do business.

Remember that this political risk may not be uniform. It will depend on the new government's needs and practices. Therefore, any nondomestic firm with products that are perceived to be necessary to the new government may receive more favorable treatment than those nondomestic companies with products not considered necessary. Also, the relationship that a nondomestic firm had with the previous government and/or the relationship with the new government will also play heavily on whether that firm is allowed to maintain business in that country. In fact, favorable relations may actually lead to more business.

Finally, all organizations doing business abroad should be aware of the fact that what they do could be the object of some political action. Thus, it is imperative that they understand that success or failure could depend on how well they cope with political decisions, and how well they anticipate changes in political attitudes and policies.

This is the framework for conducting an assessment of the political environment of an individual country:

What Is the Nature of the Political Environment?

- Who are the relevant players in the country (government vs. nongovernment)?
- Does the country exhibit all the characteristics of a functional nation-state?
- By what means is power exerted in the country (traditional monarchy, constitutional monarchy, theocracy/quasi-theocracy, constitutional republic, or Communist state)?

Specific Aspects of the Political Environment

- Extent to which a welfare state exists
- Regional development policies
- Use of fiscal vs. monetary policy
- Environmental policies
- Government enforcement of laws and regulations pertaining to business
- Extent to which power/authority is divided (e.g., national vs. regional vs. local)

Business–Government Interaction

- Does your firm and its activities represent a potential sovereignty threat?
- Does your firm and its activities have the potential to create political conflict?
- To what extent might equity and management threats (who controls the firm) be a problem?
- To what extent might earnings and performance threats (who profits from the firm) be a problem?
- To what extent might operational threats (how the firm operates) be a problem?

Assessing Political Vulnerability (Firm-Specific Issues)

- Is the firm or its products potentially involved in political debates?
- Is the firm involved in mass communication (directly or indirectly)?
- What is the potential effect of firm operations on local businesses?
- Is your product offering a service, or does it have a large service component?
- Is your product offering potentially hazardous (to individuals or society as a whole)?

THE SOCIOCULTURAL IMPERATIVE

Probably the most confusing and overlooked area for companies entering a host market is that of understanding the target country's unique culture and how it differs from their own. The task of adjusting to a new cultural environment is probably one of the biggest challenges of international business. Nondomestic firm's attempts are frequently unsuccessful because the company—either consciously or unconsciously—makes decisions or evaluations from a frame of reference that is acceptable to its home culture but unacceptable in a foreign environment. Therefore, business practices that are successful in one group of countries may be entirely inappropriate in another group of countries.

Cultural differences can make or break a business deal or relationship. This is why an attempt must be made to identify and understand cultural differences and nuances. At the heart of all of this is comfort. By your attempting to understand and deal with cultural differences, others come to understand that you are really interested in creating a relationship and, therefore, become more comfortable with the interaction. No one expects perfection, but making any attempt is a strong step in the right direction. Above all, remember that as hard as it is for you, and your firm, to understand another culture, it is as equally difficult for them to understand yours.

Finally, there is one more confounding factor when it comes to culture. Twenty-first-century culture is continuously in a state of change. Change is occurring (albeit slowly in many cases) brought on by new technology, population changes, resource scarcity and allocations, changing values regarding women's roles in many cultures, and global telecommunications. Remember that the Internet did not exist for mass consumption two decades ago and now look what it and its byproducts (blogs, text messages, emails, etc.) have done to doing business globally.

Culture is dynamic, and international firms need to regularly assess what new products and service needs have been created internationally, how different cultures are adapting to these changes, who the potential buyers and users are, and how best to reach them.

Assessing the Sociocultural Environment

The External Culture

- Material Culture: What importance is placed on the tangible?
- Social Culture: What importance is placed on intangible/human interactions?
- Natural World: What importance is placed on human–"spiritual" interactions?
- Aesthetics: What importance is placed on visual communications?
- Language: What importance is placed on verbal communications?

Culture and the Organization

- Do different value interpretations exist? Will they foster conflict?
- What is the concept of organizational structure?
- How are rewards defined/perceived?
- What are the key valued skills in this culture?

Culture and the Market

- Will the culture require a physical product change?
- Are all the products in the line relevant in this culture? Are some more/less relevant? Why?
- Are the product branding and product packaging appropriate in this market?
- What is the appropriate product positioning strategy?
- What is the perception of distribution? Is it value- or cost-added?
- How do the consumers expect to interact with a firm?

- Where do the consumers expect to find the product?
- Can the product be priced so that it is consistent with the product positioning?
- Does a country-of-origin effect exist? Is it positive or negative?

MAKING STRATEGIC DECISIONS TO ENTER AN INTERNATIONAL MARKET

There are three strategic decisions that must be made before entering a nondomestic market. First, which market, or markets, is your firm going to enter—this is the market selection problem. Second, when will your firm initiate operations in your nondomestic market(s)—this is the timing aspect of the market entry strategy problem. The timing of your market entry can be critical to success. Third, how will your firm actually enter its nondomestic market(s)—this is the actual market entry strategy your firm will adopt.

Market selection is influenced by the characteristics and stability of the market environment and your firm's ability to accurately assess your potential markets. Market entry strategy comprises three market entry choices: exporting, partnerships, and foreign direct investment. As we discussed in Chapter 6, each has its own unique set of advantages and disadvantages. However, a summary of our previous discussions related to market selection and market entry strategy raises some of the more important questions related to market selection and market entry strategy:

Which Market(s) Will Your Firm Enter?

- What about economics, politics, culture, demographics, competition, technology?
- What about projected outcomes (short-term and long-term)?
- What about prioritization?
- Which country at which time and why?

When Will Your Firm Enter This Market(s)?

- Is the market ready for you or your products?
- What is the status of your competition?
- What are the possible "first mover" advantages and disadvantages?
  Advantages: preempt competition, increase sales volume, capture market share, decrease costs, increase loyalty, may be harder for consumers to switch
  Disadvantages: pioneering costs: time, money, learning curve, educating consumers, mistakes

What Is the Scale or Scope of Your Firm's Market Entry?

- Do you want a small entry to test the waters?
- Do you plan on making a major strategic commitment?
  (Neither is totally right or wrong; it depends on your goals and situation)
- What are the primary advantages and disadvantages of exporting?
  Advantages: avoids start-up and manufacturing costs, gain experience before entering
  Disadvantages: tariffs and related costs, high transportation costs, may have higher production costs than target country
- What are the primary advantages and disadvantages of partnerships?
  Advantages: access to detailed market knowledge, access to distribution network and customers
  Disadvantages: surrendering of proprietary information, sharing of revenues
- What are the primary advantages and disadvantages of foreign direct investment?
  Advantages: assimilation into the host market, close proximity to customers, distribution network, suppliers, and competitors
  Disadvantages: high costs, high market commitment

SUMMARY

Although the international business environment is fraught with a variety of risks and threats, one means by which your firm can control for those potential problems is through the market selection process and the form of market entry strategy your firm chooses to adopt.

Appendix: A Toolkit for Developing an International Business Plan

DOING AN EXPORTING SWOT ANALYSIS

International SWOT Analysis

Also known as a "situational analysis," the goal of a SWOT analysis is to determine the current strengths and weaknesses within a firm, as well as the opportunities and threats facing your firm (SWOT = strengths, weaknesses, opportunities, threats). A SWOT analysis is used to evaluate the current position of your firm within its broader business environment. In order to be useful a SWOT analysis needs to be as honest an appraisal as possible—it is not helpful to ignore facts, exaggerate truths, or fool yourself about your firm's real circumstances. A SWOT analysis forms the foundation for strategic planning, and strategic plans, within your company.

What Does This SWOT Analysis Have to Do with International Operations?

A general SWOT analysis is essential for any planning that your firm may engage in, particularly in international operations. At some point your firm will likely need to conduct an export SWOT analysis as your international business model begins to take shape. However, this export SWOT analysis will be based to a significant extent on your general SWOT analysis. The reason why you would do a general SWOT analysis before doing a more internationally oriented SWOT analysis is that if you find your firm is threatened by new products or competitors, or if a new opportunity is identified, you may decide to *first* address the threat or take advantage of the opportunity *before* moving into any given international market.

Note: This International SWOT Checklist is not a scorecard per se but a tool for identifying both areas of strength for international operations as well as potential problem areas that must either be addressed directly or minimized through leveraging offsetting strengths. Not all aspect of this framework may apply to your specific company but you should carefully consider each before any piece is discarded or ignored.

Table 1
International SWOT Checklist

Strength/Weakness analysis	Effect for your company			Influence on performance	
	Strength	Neutral	Weakness	High	Low
1. MARKETING					
Company image					
Level of planning					
Marketing skills					
Company's reputation for quality					
Company's reputation for service					
Accessibility to raw materials					
Information availability					
Familiarity with markets					
Company's market share					
Market size					
Market growth					
Pricing strategy					
Product R&D					
New product ideas					
Marketing positioning					
Distribution strategy—domestic					
Distribution strategy—export					
Ease of entry					
Geographical proximity					
Sales force					
Advertising and promotion					

(Continued)

Table 1
International SWOT Checklist (*Continued*)

Strength/Weakness analysis	Effect for your company			Influence on performance	
	Strength	Neutral	Weakness	High	Low
2. FINANCIAL					
Cost of capital					
Financial stability					
Profitability					
Return on equity					
Debt-to-equity ratio					
3. MANUFACTURING					
Manufacturing facilities					
Economies of scale					
Capacity to increase production					
Ability to deliver on time					
Technical and manufacturing skills					
Manufacturing costs					
4. ORGANIZATIONAL					
Company's leadership					
Management aspirations for the company					
Dedication and skill of workforce					
Entrepreneurial orientation					
Flexibility and adaptability					
Staff relations					
Administration skills					
Ability to respond to changing circumstances					
Relationship with suppliers and intermediaries					
Language abilities					
Professional qualifications					

(*Continued*)

Table 1
International SWOT Checklist (*Continued*)

Strength/Weakness analysis	Effect for your company			Influence on performance	
	Strength	Neutral	Weakness	High	Low
Technical qualifications TQM environment					
Marketing knowledge					
Information management (use of it)					
Technology management					
5. DEMOGRAPHIC					
Population trends					
Age distribution					
Birth, death, and marriage rates					
Lifestyle trends					
Mobility trends					
Population's level of education					
Change in buying patterns of typical family					
6. ECONOMIC					
Growth of economy					
Size of market for products					
Rate of growth					
Foreign exchange position					
Stability of currency					
Convertibility of currency					
Per capita income					
Growth					
Income distribution					
Balance of economy					
Rate of inflation					
7. POLITICAL/LEGAL					
Stability of government					
Tariffs					
Regulations in competitive practice					

(*Continued*)

Table 1
International SWOT Checklist (*Continued*)

Strength/Weakness analysis	Effect for your company			Influence on performance	
	Strength	Neutral	Weakness	High	Low
Product labeling requirements					
Consumer information requirements					
Product standards					
Government controls					
Legislation regulating business					
Nontariff barriers					
8. SOCIAL AND CULTURAL					
Lifestyle trends					
Ethnicity of the population					
Changes in consumer tastes					
Business ethics					
Social factors in business					
Other trends					
Changes in cultural values					
9. ENVIRONMENTAL/TECHNOLOGICAL					
Importance of environmental issues					
Pace of technological change					
Innovation opportunities					
10. COMPETITION					
Dominant market players					
Number of players					
Production capacity					
11. RESEARCH AND DEVLOPMENT					
Price advantages/disadvantages					
Distribution advantages/ disadvantages					
Market segmentation					

(*Continued*)

Table 1
International SWOT Checklist (*Continued*)

Strength/Weakness analysis	Effect for your company			Influence on performance	
	Strength	Neutral	Weakness	High	Low
Product quality					
Product positioning					
Supplier power					
Customer power					
Threat of substitutions					
Threat of new entrants					
Intensity of industry rivalry					
12. EXTERNAL ENVIRONMENT					
Transportation costs					
Availability of transportation					
Distribution within the market					
Extent and reliability of communication systems					

Source: Adapted from http://www.exporthelp.co.za/index.html

Business Viability

Following the international SWOT analysis you, and your firm, should be ready to complete this Business Viability Checklist. Whereas the purpose of the SWOT analysis is to gain perspective and help to objectively focus your knowledge of your firm, this checklist serves as a scorecard for how prepared your firm is for international operations. These are questions that must be answered. As was the case with the SWOT analysis, it is important to be honest in your responses. It is generally advisable to have several individuals within your firm complete this checklist (perhaps individuals from outside the firm that are familiar enough with the firm to provide an honest evaluation as well).

In this checklist, the questions that you need to consider are listed on the left-hand side. In the "Score" column, you must give your firm a score of 1 to 10 (with 10 being the highest). Under the "Yes/No" column indicate a "yes" if you think that your firm can answer "yes" with confidence to the questions, otherwise leave it blank if it is a "no." Under the "Additional Explanation" heading you need to justify the score you have given yourself with a small explanation—you need only write down a sentence or two for the sake of clarity. At the bottom of the checklist, add up all of your scores, as well as all the "yes" answers. Your total score should at least be above 60, and you should also have a "yes" for all of the questions—if not, then you need to first focus on improving that area of operation of your current business before further developing your international business model.

Table 2
Business Viability Checklist

Questions	Score	Yes/No	Additional explanation
1. **Is your firm successful?** This is a broad judgment based on your gut feel. You are suggesting that your firm is growing, is profitable, and is cash-flush. You are able to compete against your best competitors and you have a unique product range that you sell nationally. Your firm also has areas of excellence that set your firm aside from its competitors (e.g., excellent customer services, excellent product quality, innovative products, good administration)			
2. **Are your sales growing?** If you look at your sales over the past three years, have they been growing? Is this growth better than that of your competitors? Is this growth likely to continue?			
3. **Is your firm profitable?** Do you make profits? Have you done an extensive costing exercise to identify all of your costs? Are your profits in line with those of your competitors?			
4. **Do you have a positive cash flow?** Do you regularly go into overdraft to pay for your day-to-day operations, or are you able to pay your own way? Do you currently have cash in the bank? Are most of your capital goods paid for?			

(Continued)

Table 2
Business Viability Checklist (*Continued*)

Questions	Score	Yes/No	Additional explanation
5. **Does your firm operate on a national scale in your home market?** Do you sell your goods throughout the country regularly or in one or two regions only? If you are not selling nationally, why not? Do you have branches or representatives in other parts of the country that can sell and service your products?			
6. **Does your product have unique features?** What makes your product stand out from the competition, besides for price? Is the quality exceptional? Do you have an innovative design, perhaps?			
7. **What are your firm's competitive advantages over the competition?** What aspects of your firm make it different and unique, when compared with the competition? Are you an innovative company? Are you an extremely efficient company? Are you a very good marketing company or are your product processes extremely efficient?			
8. **Has your firm exhausted all of its opportunities within the local market?** Are there unexplored opportunities still present in the home market?			
TOTAL			

If you can answer "yes" truthfully to all of these questions, then you are ready for international operations. But only then!
Source: Adapted from http://www.exporthelp.co.za/index.html

Export Readiness

Regardless of your firm's anticipated market entry strategy, prior to entering a host market, you should first determine whether or not your firm is export-ready. Exporting is the most common means of engaging in international operations and completing this Export Readiness Checklist may help to focus your market entry strategy whether or not exporting is the market entry mode selected. The checklist is divided into four parts, namely business readiness, product and production, market and marketing, and export development.

Complete this short export readiness checker to see if your company is ready or if you need to pay attention to certain areas of weakness that you may have identified as a result of this questionnaire.

Table 3
Export Readiness Checklist

Part A: Business Readiness

Question	Yes	No

Question 1
Do we know why we want to export?

Question 2
Is our company financially sound?

Question 3
Have we established that our product will be accepted internationally?

Question 4
Do we have the capacity to supply international markets?

Question 5
Are we currently selling into neighboring countries: Canada, Mexico?

Question 6
Do we have the means of communicating with an overseas buyer/distributor/agent?
Internet
Fax
Email
Telephone
Website

Question 7
Do we have a banking facility that will allow us to receive funds from our export orders, and do we have adequate finances to fund our export endeavors?

Question 8
Does our company have a suitable administration system in place?

Question 9
Can our firm advertise and promote our products in the local market?

Question 10
Is our staff sufficiently trained to carry out international trade procedures?

(*Continued*)

Table 3
Export Readiness Checklist (Continued)

Question 11
Do we have sufficient resources (staff, production, capital, and capacity) to ensure that our company can secure and maintain export orders?

Question 12
Does our company and product comply with international standards such as ISO, FDA (United States of America), CE (European Union)?

Question 13
Do we have an export plan?

Part B: Product and Production

Question	Yes	No

Question 1
Does our product compare favorably with our anticipated local competitors with regard to its features and benefits?

Question 2
Does our company have sufficient production capacity that can be committed for our export market?

Question 3
Can we maintain the consistency of the quality of the products we intend to export?

Question 4
Have we established a system to ensure the continuous supply of raw materials/inputs at the right prices, correct quality, on time?

Question 5
Do we have a system in place to ensure timely production of export orders?

Question 6
Are our production costs competitive or the same as our competitors?

Question 7
Have we given consideration to the establishment of a general or industrial rebate policy?

Question 8
Is our product new or unique in the intended export markets?

Question 9
Do we have to adapt/enhance the features of our product in order to meet or improve on the products offered by our competitors?

Question 10
Is our product required to meet specific technical and nontechnical requirements?

(Continued)

Table 3
Export Readiness Checklist (Continued)

Part C: Market and Marketing

Question	Yes	No

Question 1
Have we studied the intended markets to see if we can meet the needs and
wants of buyers better than our competition can?

Question 2
The development of an export market requires certain expertise. Have we
given attention to:
Marketing
Production
Finance/payment
Logistic
Administration

Question 3
Do we have the means of communicating with prospective international
buyers, through printed media such as advertisements, brochures, and
a website?

Question 4
Have we established what we want to say (the message) and the media that
will carry this message to the potential buyers?

Question 5
Have we identified international and local trade fair events that our company
could participate in?

Question 6
Have we determined whether we should register our company name, brand
name, or trademark in the intended market?

Question 7
Have we sufficient resources (staff, production, capital, and capacity) to
ensure that our company can achieve and maintain export orders?

Question 8
Have we identified market entry options? For example, distributors, agents,
Trading houses and/or end-users in the country of import?

Question 9
Have we a sufficient understanding of defining our risk, cost, and
responsibility in the logistic cycle?

Part D: Export Marketing

Question	Yes	No

Question 1
Do we have an indication of who our potential buyers are, or might be?

(Continued)

Table 3
Export Readiness Checklist (Continued)

Question 2
Are we aware that we may have to adapt/enhance the features of our
product/s in order to meet or better the product/s offered by other
competitors?

Question 3
Do we know if our product/s needs to meet specific technical and non
technical requirements?

Question 4
Have we identified the strengths or weaknesses related to our company
or product and/or the country of origin?

Question 5
Do we have a pricing strategy for our product that will place us in a
positive negotiating position with prospective buyers?

Source: Adapted from http://www.exporthelp.co.za/index.html

WHERE TO GET HELP

Assistance Available at the State Level

A significant amount of assistance is available at the state level to help
domestic companies to do business internationally. For example, the State of
Ohio Department of Development's (ODOD) Global Markets Division pro-
motes the export of Ohio products and services. The Global Markets Division provides companies with market research, performs agent and distributor
searches, participates in trade shows, organizes trade missions, and assists with
export finance. It also works with the Strategic Business Investment Division
to promote Ohio and attract foreign investments into the state. In addition,
Ohio has international trade offices located in Belgium, Japan, Hong Kong,
the People's Republic of China, Canada, Israel, Mexico, India, Australia,
Brazil, Chile, Argentina, and South Africa. While the programs may vary
from state to state, most offer some level of assistance to local firms exploring
the idea of engaging in international operations.

Assistance Available from the U.S. Government

Numerous resources are available from the U.S. government for companies interested in international operations. The primary government agency
dealing with international trade is the U.S. Department of Commerce and its
International Trade Administration (ITA). This organization (ITA) focuses
primarily on the exporting side of international trade. Also, the Bureau of

Export Administration (BXA) provides information on exporting regulations in various markets along with information pertaining to U.S. government export restrictions on specific products. Additionally, the U.S. Export-Import Bank provides information on financing available for exporting products and services from the United States. Other U.S. government offices providing export assistance include, but are not limited to, the U.S. Agency for International Development (USAID), the Foreign Agricultural Service (FAS), and the Office of Foreign Assets Control (OFAC).

On the importing side, a number of agencies in the U.S. Department of Commerce are responsible for providing foreign companies with information on, and regulations related to, doing business in the United States. Within the Department of Commerce's International Trade Administration is the Import Administration responsible for administering U.S. antidumping and duty laws. Additionally, the U.S. International Trade Commission (USITC) provides information on the impact of imports on U.S. industries, global trends, and updated U.S. tariff schedules. Another agency of particular value is the U.S. Treasury Department, especially the U.S. Customs Agency. U.S. Customs is the first point of contact for foreign companies doing business in the United States. Similarly, the U.S. Treasury's Office of Foreign Assets Control (OFAC) administers economic embargoes implemented by the U.S. government. Finally, the U.S. Trade Representative's Office handles trade negotiations for the U.S. government.

The above agencies and organizations are key starting points for companies considering exporting or importing products and services. In addition to the U.S. Department of Commerce, there are more than 20 U.S. government agencies that have some type and level of international trade involvement. Key among these are the U.S. Department of State, the Food and Drug Administration, the Department of Energy, and the Environmental Protection Agency. U.S. companies interested in importing/exporting can access the websites for all the above-mentioned agencies and offices for additional information and contacts.

WHAT ABOUT FOREIGN TRADE ZONES?

According to the U.S. Department of Commerce a foreign trade zone (FTZ) is defined as a site within the United States that is aligned with a U.S. Customs port of entry. As such, merchandise flowing through an FTZ is considered to be in the stream of international commerce. That is, foreign and domestic merchandise may move through the zone without a formal customs entry declaration or payment of customs duties. At the same time, such merchandise is exempt from federal and state excise/use taxes and from personal property taxes. Foreign trade zones are of two types. The general purpose zone includes multiple activities by multiple users (e.g., an industrial park). The second type, a subzone, is a one-user plant or facility.

Any international or domestic company importing or exporting products can benefit significantly from having a location in an FTZ. Key benefits include:

- deferral, reduction, and elimination of duties
- elimination of drawback
- labor overhead and profit not calculated in dutiable sale of zone merchandise
- excise tax reductions
- inventory is tax exempt while stored in an activated FTZ
- zone-to-zone transfers
- inventory control and security measures

It is a common misconception that foreign trade zones are strictly for products in-bound to the U.S. market. These FTZs can be a tremendous asset, especially as part of your international value chain, in reducing costs and increasing efficiencies. Further, FTZs are located throughout the United States, making them logistically easy to access. Any firm contemplating international operations would be well advised to identify where FTZs are located relative to its operational locations and explore how they can be leveraged in the firm's international strategies and plans.

Bibliography

Brand, Ronald A. *Fundamentals of International Business Transactions: Documents*. London: Kluwer Law International, 2000.

Capella, John J., and Stephen Hartman. *Dictionary of International Business Terms*. Hauppauge, NY: Barron's Educational Series, 2000.

Carte, Penny, and Chris Fox. *Bridging the Culture Gap: A Practical Guide to International Business Communication*. London: Kogan Page, 2007.

Cavusgil, S. Tamer, Pervez N. Ghauri, and Milind R. Agarwal. *Doing Business in Emerging Markets: Entry and Negotiation Strategies*. Thousand Oaks, CA: Sage, 2002.

Curry, Jeffrey E. *A Short Course in International Marketing: Approaching and Penetrating the Global Marketplace*. Petaluma, CA: World Trade Press, 1998.

Delphos, William A. *Inside the World Bank Group: The Practical Guide for International Business Executives*. Cary, NC: Oxford University Press USA, 2011.

DiMatteo, Larry. *The Law and International Business Transactions*. Cincinnati, OH: South-Western College Publications, 2002.

Ferraro, Gary P. *The Cultural Dimension of International Business*. Upper Saddle River, NJ: Prentice-Hall, 2001.

Folsom, Ralph H., Michael W. Gordon, and John A. Spanogle. *International Business Transaction: In a Nutshell*. Eagan, MN: West Group Publishing, 2000.

Ghauri, Pervez N., and Jean-Claude Usunier. *International Business Negotiations*. Oxford, England: Elsevier Science, 2003.

Goldstein, Morris, Carmen Reinhart, and Graciela Kaminsky. *Assessing Financial Vulnerability: An Early Warning System for Emerging Markets*. Washington, DC: Institute for International Economics, 2000.

Gomory, Ralph E., and William J. Baumol. *Global Trade and Conflicting National Interests*. Cambridge, MA: MIT Press, 2001.

Griffin, John P. *International Sales and the Middleman: Managing Your Agents and Distributors*. New York: Management Books, 1991.

Gundling, Ernest. *Working Globesmart: 12 People Skills for Doing Business across Borders*. Pasadena, CA: Davies-Black Publications, 2003.

Hugos, Michael H. *Essentials of Supply Chain Management*. Hoboken, NJ: Wiley & Sons, 2002.

Iqbal, M. Zafar. *International Accounting: A Global Perspective*. Cincinnati, OH: South-Western College Publications, 2001.

Marx, Elisabeth. *Breaking through Culture Shock: What You Need to Succeed in International Business*. London: Nicholas Brealey Intercultural, 2001.

Nelson, Carl A. *Import/Export: How to Get Started in International Trade*. Columbus, OH: McGraw-Hill, 2000.

Pooler, Victor H., David J. Pooler, and Samuel D. Farney. *Global Purchasing and Supply Management: Fulfill the Vision*. London: Kluwer Academic Publishing, 2004.

Quelch, John A., and Rohit Deshpande. *The Global Market: Developing a Strategy to Manage across Borders*. Hoboken, NJ: Jossey-Bass, 2004.

Rockwell, Browning. *Using the Web to Compete in a Global Marketplace*. Hoboken, NJ: Wiley & Sons, 1998.

Root, Franklin R. *Entry Strategies for International Markets*. Hoboken, NJ: Jossey-Bass, 1998.

Schadewald, Michael S., and Robert J. Misey. *Practical Guide to U.S. Taxation of International Transactions*. London: Kluwer Business Publications, 2009.

Schultz, Don E., and Philip J. Kitchen. *Communicating Globally: An Integrated Marketing Approach*. Columbus, OH: McGraw-Hill, 2000.

Sherman, Andrew J. *Franchising and Licensing: Two Powerful Ways to Grow Your Business in Any Economy*. Chicago: American Marketing Association, 2003.

Tuller, Lawrence W. *Exporting, Importing, and Beyond: How to "Go Global" with Your Small Business*. Avon, MA: Adams Media Corp, 1997.

U.S. Department of Commerce. *A Basic Guide to Exporting*. Columbus, OH: McGraw-Hill. 1996.

Van Gelder, Sicco. *Global Brand Strategy: Unlocking Brand Potential across Countries, Cultures, and Markets*. London: Kogan Page, 2003.

Venedikian, Harry M., and Gerald A. Warfield. *Global Trade Financing*. Hoboken, NJ: Wiley & Sons, 2000.

Wallace, Robert. *Strategic Partnerships: An Entrepreneur's Guide to Joint Ventures and Alliances*. Dearborn, MI: Dearborn Trade, 2004.

Williams, Mark A. *The 10 Lenses: Your Guide to Living and Working in a Multicultural World*. Wellington, NJ: Capital Books, 2001.

Index

investments, 96; intellectual property protection inefficiencies, 46; non-market government environment, 39; nonmarket nongovernment environment, 39–40; political process in, 39–40, 44; presence of McDonald's, 115; restrictions placed on technology, information transfer, 47

The Coca-Cola Company, 29

Communication: challenges of differing value systems, 59; commercial communications, 58; facilitation strategies, 125, 127; global advances, 34; interactive communications, 104, 134–41; mass communications, 48, 50; message standardization, 141–48; promotional communications, 63, 131; selectivity problems, 132–34; visual tools, 121; written communications, 75

Communist state political system, 44

Competitive advantage: assessment of, 28–29, 78; considerations, in business plan, 151–52, 154, 162; consumer preferences and, 144; dangers of partnerships, 14; of governments, 45; licensing and, 90; possible costs of, 8; question of achievability, 7

Competitive environment assessment, 26–33; creating market perception, 31; hypercompetition, 27; pre-assessment questions, 32–33; sources of advantages, 27–28; strengths assessment, 29–30; threats from local firms, 26–27; weaknesses assessment, 30

Concept determination (of products), 116–17

Constitutional monarchy political system, 43

Constitutional republic political system, 43–44

Consumers: Chinese consumers, 39; competitive environment assessment, 28–29, 33; cultural differences, 7; economic environment assessment, 23–26; efforts made for

buying, 10; ethical issues, 8; Foster's Lager example, 11–12; Japan/disposable diaper example, 16–17; McDonald's example, 13; and product saturation, 15–16

Cost-benefit analysis, 8, 11

Cultural/social environment (of markets), 5

Culture: aesthetics/language, 58–59; defined, 53–55; enforced aspects, 55; as foundational to human interaction, 53; human-spiritual interactions, 57–58; ingredients of, 56–59; and international business, 59–62; learning aspects, 54; and market activities, 62–64; material-based culture, 56, 58, 59–60; organizational approach, 61–62; overlap of demographics, 20; process-based approaches, 60–61; relation of the social imperative, 53–64; shared aspects, 54–55; social culture, 56–57; values-grounded culture, 60

Customer connections. See Value chain creation (connecting with customers)

Demographic environment assessment, 20–23; approach to, 20–21; macro level approach, 21–22; micro level approach, 22; profile development, 22–23

Demographics (defined), 20

Design strategy, of products: market development considerations, 119; market environment considerations, 119–21; "standardizable" product characteristics, 121; standardization vs. customization, 118

Dictator-state political system, 42

Domestic extension strategy: components of success, 10; described, 9; vs. global strategy, 12–13; vs. multidomestic strategy, 11

Dunlop brand tires, 92

Economic assessment, for business plan, 160–62

About the Author

BRUCE D. KEILLOR is an associate professor of marketing and international business at Youngstown State University in Youngstown, Ohio. In addition to being a recognized scholar in international business he is a consultant to Fortune 500 firms and a successful entrepreneur.